PRAISE FOR JIM HEFFERNAN:

"Every newspaper needs a storyteller and Jim Heffernan served his native city and the *Duluth News Tribune* well. He wrote about those living in the Northland and those who touched them from the era of Buddy Holly, Elvis Presley and John F. Kennedy to the present. Heffernan's columns were a slice of unique humor and insight."

— KEVIN PATES, *DULUTH NEWS TRIBUNE* SPORTSWRITER
(AND POP CULTURE AFICIONADO)

"Returning to my hometown Duluth over the ~~...~~
pleasure in reading Jim's column. J~~...~~
member of the family, and findin~~...~~
and the occasional absurdities of th~~...~~ wn
was still essentially the same, and ~~...~~ ands."

— RICK SHEFCHIK, AUTHOR OF THE "SA~~...~~ARDA" MYSTERIES
Amen Corner AND *Green Monster*.

"Jim has become the unofficial historian of Duluth's role in the last days before 'The Day the Music Died' when singer Buddy Holly appeared here shortly before he and others were killed in a plane crash. I sponsored and emcee'd the show; Jim was there and has written movingly about it."

— LEW LATTO, VETERAN DULUTH RADIO TALK SHOW HOST
(AND BROADCAST EXECUTIVE)

"They say laughter is the best medicine. If that's the case, Jim Heffernan left a lot of people healthy with his *News Tribune* columns. Amidst the headlines of crime and mayhem Heffernan's column brought a dose of light-hearted humor that lifted the spirits and always made it a better day. His droll sense of humor and easy wit often made me laugh out loud."

— BARBARA REYELTS, NEWS MANAGER, *Northland's NewsCenter*

"Jim Heffernan's columns have moved us to laughter and tears, troubled our conscience, confronted our humanity, and made us recognize ourselves through the lens of these gifted verbal sketches."

— JIM OBERSTAR, U.S. CONGRESSMAN REPRESENTING NORTHEASTERN MINNESOTA

Cooler Near the Lake

Fifty-two Favorites from
Thirty-four Years of Deadlines

JIM HEFFERNAN

DULUTH, MINNESOTA

X-communication
Duluth, Minnesota
www.x-communication.org
218-310-6541

Cooler near the lake:
fifty-two favorites from thirty-four years of deadlines

Cover and interior design and layout by Tony Dierckins.
Cover and back cover photos by Ken Moran.
Proof reading by Suzanne Rauvola.

The stories in this volume were originally published
in the *Duluth News-Tribune,* the *Duluth Herald,*
the *Duluth News-Tribune & Herald*, and the *Duluth News Tribune.*
and are reprinted here with permission.

First Edition, 2008
08 09 10 11 12 • 5 4 3 2 1

Library of Congress Control Number: 2008935822
ISBNs: 1-887317-34-1 & 978-1-887317-34-4

Printed in Brainerd, Minnesota, U.S.A., by Bang Printing.

With love for Voula,
who never blanched at the outrageous nonsense.

— J.H.

CONTENTS

PART IV: THE ETHNIC EDITOR

PART V: THE RICH & FAMOUS COLLIDE WITH DULUTH

PART VI: THROUGH THE REARVIEW MIRROR

PREFACE

*T*his collection has been a long time coming. It might never have come if my association with the *Duluth News Tribune* hadn't ended in June 2008 after more than three decades of column writing for that paper and the late *Duluth Herald*. (In 1982 the papers were combined as the *Duluth News-Tribune & Herald*; in 1988 the publisher dropped "*&* *Herald*" from the name; the hyphen between "News" and "Tribune" was dropped in 2000.)

After the first few years of writing columns for the Duluth dailies, I'd get asked from time to time when (if?) a collection of columns would be coming out in book form. I always played it coy, saying maybe someday, but then never pursued it. As the years went by, I had moments of hoping a publisher would call and suggest such a volume. A couple of years ago, Tony Dierckins of Duluth's X-Communication did just that. I put him off then, but in summer 2008 we revived the idea and this book is the happy result.

It contains 52 (symbolically one for each week in a year) columns from the approximately 1,500 I wrote between 1973 and 2008. It was challenging to choose 52 from so many, but doing so brought back a lot of memories. Reading some I'd forgotten made me wince at times, others made me smile and a few others made me feel proud that I'd written them. I tried to keep the "made me wince" columns out of this book, and hope I've succeeded.

Throughout the years, I've thought of myself as a "humor columnist," hoping readers would agree. Humor writing is a shot in the dark, though. People's perceptions of what's funny and what isn't vary so widely that one person's belly laugh is another's bellyache. Still, the encouragement of readers who took the trouble to write and say this-or-that column cheered them during tough times in their lives was extremely gratifying. So this book contains lots of columns written strictly for laughs, many in the chapter I've titled "Outrageous Nonsense," because that is what they are.

It was interesting to me to discover that I wrote as many serious columns as I did, usually associated with life's milestones. Several are included in the chapter titled "Slices of Life." Discovering them again—kids' high school graduations, Christmases past, the death of a beloved dog—gave me pause as the memories came flooding back. These are experiences most of us have, and I hope mine reflect the emotions we all feel at these times.

When I began as a columnist there were no other local or "signed" columns in the Duluth paper, aside from those in the sports section. I told the newspaper's editor I thought the paper would benefit from a local column, and he decided to give me a try. I was warned, though, that it's awfully hard, even burdensome, to come up with something week after week, and it is, but it's a wonderful challenge, too. I always considered it my form of gambling.

I must acknowledge the several people who made all this possible. That executive editor who agreed to let me try a column was Orville E. "Bud" Lomoe, who passed away in 1991. I doubt he ever imagined it would last for a full generation and then some.

This book's publisher, Tony Dierckins, is mentioned above. He's much more than a publisher (and editor). He's an enthusiastic, energetic, optimistic Duluthian whose encouragement has made this project a pleasure.

The preparation and processing of the manuscript, together with perceptive suggestions on content, became job No. 1 for my wife, Voula, whose dedication and mastery of the Mac made this collection possible.

I appreciate the cooperation of the *Duluth News Tribune* and its executive editor, Rob Karwath, for granting rights to reprint this material and access to the newspaper's archives to retrieve a number of columns stored there. BreAnn Graber, the editor's administrative assistant, cheerfully dug columns out of the paper's electronic archives for use in this collection.

Veteran Duluth photographer Ken Moran suggested the cover photo and traipsed to the Park Point beach on a warm day to capture the lake effect suggested in the title, "Cooler Near the Lake." It wasn't cool that day, but Ken's work was, and it's appreciated.

Duluthian Patricia Daugherty led all the rest in pressing me to collect my columns in a book, and I thank her for her persistence.

Finally, none of this would ever have been possible without the support of my family throughout the years: Voula, of course, but our daughter, Kate, and son, Patrick, as well. They were the inspiration for more columns than they realize.

— Jim Heffernan, September 2008

PART I:

THE LAKE EFFECT

THE LAKE EFFECT

W hy title this opening chapter "Lake Effect"? Well, Lake Superior, more than anything else, dominates our lives here at the Head of the Lakes—especially our weather. Our great lake's effect on our weather was the inspiration for the most popular column, in terms of reader reaction, of all 1,500 or so that I have written for the Duluth newspapers.

Thus, "Cooler Near the Lake" is this book's title and the opening column of this section. It isn't really a column, but rather a bit of doggerel that some call "poetry." It was great fun to write, and the wonderful reaction of readers has been gratifying. To this day, I occasionally hear from people who find it clipped out of the paper among the effects of loved-ones after they have passed on. So here it is, one last time.

Columns in the rest of this section also reflect life in Duluth—including more on Duluth's weather. "Summertime: Another Day, Another Storm" was written during a wet period when it seemed like we got a storm a day, and "Old Man Winter's Gone Looking for a Natural High" is a take on a particularly warm February.

Others in this section reflect other aspects of life here, and one, "Plastic Deer Threatened in City Hunt," written in mock news form, was actually believed by some readers both here and elsewhere in the country (via the Internet), and caused quite a stir. The smelt-fishing season is revived here, too, if not on our lake, and don't ask which six funerals are needed for Duluth to really prosper.

The rest of the columns in this section speak for themselves, all reflecting aspects of life in Duluth, including the dominance of hockey—in season, when it's really cooler near the lake.

COOLER NEAR THE LAKE

They say we're in God's country,
And few could argue that,
With forests tall and waters blue
And folks who'll go to bat.
But one thing gets my dander up,
Beyond just give and take,
And that's the report on the radio
That it's cooler near the lake.

It happens every springtime,
And in the summer too,
Just when buds are popping
And the skies are getting blue,
When the world embraces sunshine
And our bones for warmth all ache,
It's then you know the reports will show
That it's cooler near the lake.

It's only here, and nowhere else,
That such a case is true;
In nearby towns and villages,
There's no need there to rue;
They get the balmy breezes,
They're out with hoe and rake,
But in Duluth, you know it's the truth,
It'll be cooler near the lake.

Just take a ride to Hermantown,
Or Hibbing or Virginia;
Go down to Minneapolis
If you think you've got it in ya.
You'll find that they are basking
In the heat, make no mistake,
But in Duluth, you know, forsooth,
It'll be cooler near the lake.

I sometimes think the weather here
Will never get past fifty;
If it happens to rise to sixty-five
Everyone thinks it's nifty;
By afternoon you can bet your boots,
If you don't you'll be a fake,
By eventide the temp will slide,
And it'll be cooler near the lake.

We love our lake, don't get me wrong,
Its gorgeous shining water,
But looks are only surface deep,
There are other things that matter;
Like warming bones that winter froze,
And limbs that quiver and quake,
Fat chance we've got to heat 'em up
When it's cooler near the lake.

It's not as though we don't get warned
By all those darn forecasters;
I swear each night, as they give our plight,
That they're no-good dirty _ _ _ _ _ _ _ _.
They say the same thing every time
When they describe our fate:
We're sorry folks, and it's no joke,
It'll be cooler near the lake.

I know the day is coming when
The real God's Country beckons,
And when St. Peter meets me there,
He'll ask my home, I reckon.
And when I tell him it's Duluth
He'll say, "For heaven's sake,
Ain't that the place everyone says
Is cooler near the lake?"

"That's it," I'll cry, "oh kindly saint,
And in this realm please spare,
From chilly off-lake breezes,
And winter underwear."
"If it's heat you want," he'll reply,
In the other place you'll bake."
"Fine, send me any place except
Where it's cooler near the lake!"

Originally appeared in the Duluth News-Tribune *on Sunday, June 3, 1979.*

SUMMERTIME:
ANOTHER DAY, ANOTHER STORM

Summertime, when the livin' is easy…

*H*o, hum. It does get a little monotonous in summer. Every day becomes like the one before it in a steady succession of summertime routine.

You wake up to the tune of tornado sirens blaring and the clock radio blasting warnings of impending danger.

You climb out of bed and quickly throw on some clothes so that you won't be too embarrassed when they find your body.

You hastily close the windows of your house to avoid sheets of rain coming in and shrinking your carpets.

You glance skyward out the window and see dark clouds roiling above as though it were the end of the world.

Lightning flashes in the sky over your house and tumultuous thunder follows immediately, indicating that the center of the storm is exactly where you are.

You tune in your radio to the weather service frequency where personnel are issuing urgent instructions on what to do and what not to do (do not get on a "down" elevator if the basement is full of water, etc.).

You turn on the cable TV weather channel and on-air personalities are concerned about a "tropical low" heading toward Bermuda, although across the bottom of the screen local conditions are written out telling persons in St. Louis, Carlton, Douglas, Bayfield and Washburn counties, and anyone on the open waters of Lake Superior, to get their affairs in order.

You make your way to the southwest corner of your basement and huddle in the fetal position on the cold concrete floor, mumbling prayers imploring the Almighty to spare you.

Your electricity fails and two or three trees blow down in your yard.

Your lawn furniture disappears from your deck and afterward you find it sticking out of the windshield of your neighbor's car.

Your dog announces he is moving to Canada.

Fifteen minutes later the storm subsides and you emerge from the basement and begin resetting all of your clocks.

You decide to venture outside, and find the temperature and humidity are so high that cattle and turkeys are dropping in their tracks. Overheated radio announcers recite warnings about becoming overheated, recommending the public drink plenty of liquids.

You resolve to stop drinking plenty of solids.

You catch a bus and as you ride through neighborhoods you see trees and branches strewn in yards and on roadways.

You get off at Duluth's Karpeles Manuscript Museum and offer to sign a last will and testament for them to display, but they turn you down because you are not George Washington.

Later, you go for a walk in a remote clearing where aliens swoop down in a saucer-like space vehicle, take you aboard, give you a complete physical examination, tell you your cholesterol is high, and hand you a bill for $595 and change.

For supper you decide to cook outdoors on your kettle grill, and, upon opening it, you find it contains a dead raccoon with a yellow stripe up its back.

You hit the sack about midnight, noting a near-full moon is brightly shining and stars are twinkling. Not a cloud in the sky.

About seven hours later, the tornado warning goes off and you begin the whole routine all over again.

Summer can be a boring time.

Originally appeared in the Duluth News-Tribune *on Sunday, July 16, 1995.*

PLASTIC DEER THREATENED IN CITY HUNT

*H*ere's the latest fair and balanced news...

Homeowners who decorate their yards with life-sized plastic deer are complaining the sculptures are being damaged by people stalking real deer during Duluth's special season for bowhunters.

"My decorative doe, Felicity, had an arrow sticking out of her hind quarter," Orval Pussywillow of Hunter's Park complained yesterday. "This has got to stop. We paid good money for our beautiful deer." Pussywillow said his four plastic pink flamingos and a lawn ornament depicting the posterior of a fat woman bending over were unmolested.

Local police said they have received numerous complaints from throughout the city that plastic deer are being shot with arrows by hunters mistaking them for the real thing. One citizen, who declined to be identified "because I work with a bowhunter," said she has outfitted her plastic deer with blaze orange vests to protect them from arrows.

Randy Waxwing, spokesman for the Lake Superior Spear, Boomerang & Bowhunters Ltd., said residents with plastic deer in their yards should remove them from now through season's end December 31st to protect them during the municipal bowhunting season. "You can't blame our people for shooting plastic deer; they're so lifelike. Many of our own members have plastic deer themselves as inspiration for hunting season. Hunters love deer; that's why we kill them."

Waxwing did point out that association members are complaining to him that their hunting arrows are being blunted by hitting plastic deer and not the soft flesh of real deer. "It's a two-way street," he said. "Good hunting arrows cost plenty."

Thelma Twelvetrees of Thelma's Yard, Garden and Southern Belle Figurine Emporium, which sells ornamental deer, said sales are down since the city bowhunting season was announced. "People don't want to fork over good money for plastic deer only to have them shot full of arrows," she said. It was not known how the decline in faux deer sales would affect city sales tax receipts.

Meanwhile, Msgr. Ernest X. Chasuble said religious leaders are concerned that fake donkeys in Christmas nativity scenes will be shot at by hunters when churches erect crèches on their lawns beginning around Thanksgiving. "Also wise men riding camels. What if they hit a wise man? Or the Holy Mother, for that matter?" Chasuble asked.

Concern about safety around Christmas crèches outside local churches was seconded by Worship Duluth, successor organization to the Duluth Church and Sunday School Bureau, in a news release. "The Christmas message of 'Peace on Earth' is diluted when you find arrows sticking in outdoor religious displays," the news release stated. Religious leaders said either the hunt should be suspended during the holidays or characters in the displays should be adorned with blaze orange garments.

Officials also predict that ornamental reindeer in secular home displays will be affected.

Finally, Professor Michael Angelo, head of the Sculpture and Human Sexuality Department at the Arrowhead College of Carnal Knowledge, said plastic ornamental deer are an important part of American art on a par with department store mannequins. "I once saw a fake deer with a nude female mannequin astride it. Priceless," said Angelo, 43, who is registered with the police.

Film at 10.

Originally appeared in the Duluth News Tribune *on Sunday, September 25, 2005.*

SMELT MEMORIES: ARE THEY FACT OR FANCY?

Where's the smelt?

Somebody asked me the other night when I was going to write my annual smelt column, and I had to admit that I hadn't even thought of doing one this year. Maybe I forgot because the smelt forgot to come.

I'm getting the impression in recent years that the smelt themselves are tired of the annual ritual. They seem to be looking elsewhere for their spring kicks.

As many of us who remember the halcyon days of smelting know, it wasn't always that way. Newcomers to Duluth would have difficulty understanding what mania the arrival of the smelt used to cause back in the early days of smelt running.

I was attempting to describe it to someone who recently moved to Duluth and I found myself doubting what I was saying. I had that eerie feeling one sometimes gets that I had dreamed it all, and then confused the dream with reality.

So I thought I'd check myself with readers who might have the same memories as mine.

Is it a fact, or is it fantasy, when I seem to recall that Park Point, and not the North Shore, was the focus of the smelt run in the early days? Didn't thousands of people used to converge on the Point during the run and fish with huge net seines? And wasn't there a bonfire, often fueled with old tires, about every 20 feet for the length of the Point?

I was pretty young, but I remember looking across the lake from a location near Leif Erikson Park and seeing so many bonfires on the beach that it looked like all of Park Point was on fire. What happened to that? I'm only asking.

And when the weather was rough on the lake side of the Point, didn't the multitudes shift over to the bay side with their seines, some substituting dip nets, and wade far out into harbor waters—almost to the ship channels—in search of smelt? I remember doing that once on a smelt excursion with my father. I think I remember it, or was it a dream?

Do I recall that you didn't need a Minnesota fishing license, no matter what your age, to smelt fish? Didn't that bring just about every man, woman and child in Minnesota and the four states surrounding it to Duluth? Didn't they cause traffic jams on London Road extending from the Lester River to the Jay Cooke statue? Did that happen, or was it just that I was younger and everything seemed bigger then?

Didn't roving bands of young people get drunked up on 3.2 beer and pillage, if not rape, everything in sight? Weren't enough empty beer cans strewn along the shore and Park Point to provide sufficient metal to build three destroyers and a battlewagon?

Weren't the police put on double duty to make a stab at keeping order, and the traffic moving, and didn't they always lose the battle? Did the Chamber of Commerce hook up a statewide smelt information alert line for outstate people to call for up-to-the-minute reports on the smelt run, or did I dream that?

Didn't the *Duluth Herald* and the *Duluth News-Tribune* (there were two papers then) composing room overnight smelting party at Lester River each year turn every printer into a devil, and cause four-score worried wives to sit up all night in rocking chairs at home clutching rosaries and praying? Did I imagine all that?

Speaking of the newspaper, didn't each edition come out with four-column pictures of the hordes at Lester River, and didn't occasional 84-point (War Declared-size) headlines announce that some men had given up their lives in pursuit of smelt. That happened, didn't it?

Didn't I see a neighbor lady come home from smelting and dump huge buckets of smelt directly into her garden for fertilizer? Wasn't the peak of the run the biggest night of the year for the liquor stores—eclipsing New Year's?

I'm not complaining that all this appears to have come to an end, mind you. I'm only asking if it really happened the way I recall it, or was it all a dream?

Originally appeared in the Duluth News-Tribune & Herald *on Wednesday, May 9, 1984.*

OLD MAN WINTER'S GONE LOOKING FOR A NATURAL HIGH

*T*he memo came down to detectives about mid-morning. It was from the chief.

"Report to my office at 1 P.M. sharp," it was tersely worded.

"What do you suppose the chief wants?" the detective inspector asked.

"Beats me," said the sergeant.

The whole detective bureau staff was assembled in its dingy office. Some of the officers were tired from the night before after a stakeout at a skating rink.

"This must be serious," another detective said. "The chief wouldn't call us all in unless it was big. Maybe a drug bust or burglary ring or something."

The detectives could hardly wait until 1 P.M. to find out what the chief wanted. Finally the hour came and they filed into the chief's office. The chief looked troubled and stern.

"We've got the biggest missing person case in the history of this city," the chief opened. "We're going to have to go at this full bore. Every person on the force will be on it and I will direct it myself."

The detectives were troubled. "Chief, who is it, the mayor?" asked the inspector. "Is it one of the city council members? Who's missing, chief?"

"Old Man Winter," the chief grimaced. "He's been gone for close to a week. We've got to find him. It's the biggest challenge this department has ever faced. Now I want everybody out on the streets. Talk to all of your informers. Scour the parks and golf courses. Somebody cover the waterfront. Check the hospitals. Get an APB out on the wire. I want Old Man Winter found in 24 hours or heads will roll."

The chief meant it, too. After all, it was mid-February. Skating rinks were closing; cross-country skiing was impossible; snowmobiles were inert in pools of water in a thousand back yards; bicycles were starting to show up on city streets; people were sunning themselves on porches; lovers were necking on scenic overlooks; pedestrians were walking the streets without coats.

"Look out there," the chief continued, pointing to the window. "It looks like April in a good year. We've got to track down Old Man Winter or your name will be mud."

"We'll get right on it, Chief," said the detective inspector. "You can count on us."

That evening, after the sun went down, they got a break in the case. A pair of plainclothes officers picked up Jack Frost coming out of a sleazy bar in the bowery, staggering down the street as though he were on his last legs. They threw him in a squad and brought him to headquarters for the third degree under the lights. The inspector took charge.

"All right Frost, where's the Old Man? Tell us or we'll stay here until you melt down to nothing," the cop barked. They all knew Frost was slippery.

"Why do you think I got drunk?" Frost pleaded. "I don't know where Old Man Winter went. If I did I'd bring him back myself. You think I like this?" He started to sob, icicles running on his cheeks.

"When did you last see Old Man Winter?" another detective asked.

"Last week. We were up to Mother Nature's house. The Old Man and I went up there to fool around, you know, with some of Mother Nature's girls, Daisy, Blossom and the others. I had a little too much ice and passed out. Next thing I knew I was out in the warm, almost melting down. I ain't seen the Old Man since."

"So Mother Nature's involved, eh?" said the inspector. "Pick her up."

A squad found Mother Nature walking the streets, laughing as though she'd gone crazy. After placing her in the squad they couldn't shut her up as they drove to headquarters—she just kept laughing and laughing.

"What are you laughing at?" one of the patrolmen asked her.

"You know Old Man Winter?" Mother Nature said. "He ran off and got married, and you know who he married? My girl Spring, that's who."

"That's funny?" asked the other cop.

"It sure is, because I told him not to marry Spring. She's too young and fickle for him. He'll never be able to keep her. I know that old codger. He'll be back next week, bellowing all over the place. You'll see."

When the officers told the chief what Mother Nature said, the investigation was called off. "The Old Man shouldn't have done it," the chief said, "you know it's not nice to fool Mother Nature."

Originally appeared in the Duluth Herald *on Thursday, February 19, 1981.*

STILL WAITING FOR FUNERALS IN EAST END

When I was a child growing up in Duluth's friendly West End, I recall hearing it said, "What Duluth needs is six good funerals." Not very friendly, if you ask me.

Still, it's understandable that you'd hear such a thing in the West End since all of the funerals would have taken place in Duluth's wealthy East End.

Kids from the West End at this time—we're talking the 1950s—assumed that everyone in the East End of Duluth was rich and no one in the West End was, an assumption that was largely true, but not entirely. We had a neighbor who actually drove Chryslers very fast, like Marie Antoinette's coachman, and if a child had been hit, the victim's family could eat cake.

Such attitudes can lead to revolutions, but not here. All that came out of it was that "What Duluth needs is six good funerals," not including the guy in the Chrysler.

I suppose I should explain to the newly arrived (25 years or less) that the reason it was believed we needed these half dozen funerals was that the individuals—who remained unnamed—hoarded all of the money and blocked the paths of others seeking to increase their fortunes. This, in turn, prevented Duluth itself from living up to its potential as the colossus of the Midwest, eclipsing even Chicago. Minneapolis? Forget about it.

I can't be sure, but I've heard that the phrase might have been coined in the East End—by none other than the famous author Sinclair Lewis. He lived in a mansion in that part of Duluth for just under two years shortly after World War II with his girlfriend and her mother.

As I grew older the refrain about Duluth needing six good funerals continued, although you'd assume that at least one or two of the funerals had already been held, and that Lewis should marry the girl. He never did.

After completing my education and taking a job in the world of journalism at the *Duluth Herald* and the *Duluth News Tribune* (the *Herald*'s funeral was held 25 years ago), I was able to observe the local establishment from closer range. As a reporter you must consort with the locally high and mighty from time to time at the professional level, but not the social.

I'd find myself wondering at such times if some of the people I met were among those said to be in need of a funeral, perhaps even one of the Zenith City Six.

As fate or lack of ambition (I'm never sure) would have it, I stayed in Duluth for my entire career, working in various aspects of journalism here at this newspaper. Throughout those years, I'd hear from time to time that to progress, Duluth needed about six funerals, and wonder how the old skinflints in need of funerals were surviving so long.

Now I am retired from active journalism, only continuing as a columnist. From the beginning until now some 44 years have passed, but the other day it came up again: "What Duluth needs is six good funerals."

Boy, those rich guys from the East End sure are hanging on.

Originally appeared in the Duluth News Tribune *on Sunday, April 22, 2007.*

WHEN THE TOWER TALKS, EVERYBODY LISTENS

*I*f you stop for a moment and listen, the wind will talk to you as it blows past Enger Tower.

There is always a wind at the top of Duluth's West End hill where the tower has kept a vigil for 41 years. Maybe the crews that are now engaged in cleaning up the landmark for the first time since it was built can hear the voices.

The tower has heard a lot over the more than four decades it has looked down on the city from the windswept heights, and if you ever go up there alone you can hear it too.

It isn't commonly known, but anything said on the tower is forever captured by it and whispered back to the wind, only to be repeated when a person stands at the top alone, facing the breeze. Many people foolishly have taken a shot at immortality by carving or painting names, words or thoughts on its granite and concrete walls or weatherbeaten woodwork.

They needn't have bothered.

Now the cleanup and refinishing crews are expunging the graffiti and all that will remain are the voices, forever etched in the wind and whispered back by the breeze that sweeps across Lake Superior and is momentarily sliced by the formidable bastion before it continues its journey inland.

If you listen carefully, you can hear the voices, perhaps even your own from some bygone day when the tower played a role in your life as it has at one time or another in the lives of most Duluthians.

You can hear the laughing voices of children counting the steps to the top. You can hear the giggling of teen-age boys and girls, many in the throes of first love, hesitatingly expressing their feelings. You can hear the exclamations of tourists, marveling at the magnificent view. You can hear the jeering voices of destructive youths, trying to bend the bars on its windows, breaking empty bottles against its inside walls, or carving or writing graffiti on every flat surface.

The tower doesn't care.

It doesn't care if fires are lit inside it. Granite and concrete don't burn. It doesn't care about the graffiti—it learned all the bad words long ago. It doesn't care about the broken glass that is scattered throughout its stairwells.

Through it all, the tower stands and just listens and it knows that as far as it is concerned, nothing will ever change. There will be more vandals and more graffiti. And there will be more children and lovers and tourists. It welcomes every new generation at every stage of its life and quietly listens and perseveres.

It's seen times of depression and war and times of tranquility. They all come and go just like the people, but the tower never changes. If it could be destroyed it would have happened long ago.

A hundred—who knows, maybe a thousand—years from now when all of us who have ever used or abused the tower in some way in our lifetimes are long gone, the tower will still be there playing host to that generation's children, lovers, vandals and tourists.

If Enger Tower symbolizes anything, it is simply this: If you could build it big enough and tough enough, all the beating and burning and smashing and kicking and carving and gouging won't really hurt it.

There's nothing very noble about that, but it's something.

Originally appeared in the Duluth Herald *on Thursday, May 15, 1980.*

The Game of Hockey
Is a Lot Like Life—Stupid

*H*eaven knows I try to keep up with what's going on when I watch hockey, but it's a fast game, and most of the time I don't know why the referee or linesman or other guy in a striped shirt blows the whistle, so I ask somebody and when they tell me I feel stupid.

I didn't grow up playing or watching hockey and never paid that much attention to the rules of the game, so with hockey it's like I'm from China or Mars or somewhere. I don't know things other men seem to know about the game and when I ask and they have to tell me I feel stupid.

Oh, it's pretty easy to follow hockey in a surface way—bunch of skaters in dark jerseys try to maneuver the puck past a bunch of skaters in light jerseys and put it in a mesh net protected by a "goaltender." But a lot can happen along the way, and when they blow the whistle to stop the action I don't know why so I have to ask somebody and when they tell me I feel stupid.

Or if they don't stop the game, but the other people in the crowd begin to holler at the ref that he missed something I missed but I don't know what he missed, I feel stupid.

It's easy for guys who have been patrons of the game of hockey all their lives to recognize infractions of the rules, but how's somebody like me who doesn't know cross checking from butt ending supposed to know when they're doing it? Then, if I ask somebody, I feel stupid.

I'm getting better. I used to wonder about things like "off side" and "icing" and when I'd ask someone what happened ("Why'd they blow the whistle?"), they'd explain what an off side is or what icing is and when I didn't really catch on they'd think I'm stupid.

But I've got those down good now—so good that, when I see the puck go all the way from one end of the ice to the other and the official blows his whistle, I mutter "icing" to the person next to me who gives me a look that has "so what else is new?" written all over it, and I feel stupid.

Same thing with "off sides." After years of inquiring, I finally learned that they're off side when the skater crosses the "blue" line ahead of the puck, so I'm pretty quick to show off my knowledge by hollering "off side" when it happens, but nobody else does because it's so obvious and then I feel stupid.

After years of watching hockey games, I still have trouble figuring out which penalties are which. The referee has certain hand signals that other people recognize as signals for such offenses as high sticking, hooking or slashing, but I don't know which signal is which, and when I have to ask somebody what the penalty was, I feel stupid.

I don't think I'll ever really understand what they mean by "forechecking" but sometimes when I watch the game on TV and they interview a sweaty, breathless player at the end and ask him, "What was it that turned the game around for you guys?" and the player says, "We forechecked well," I always wonder how I could have watched a whole game and not noticed, and right there in my living room I feel stupid.

Hockey announcers are always making me feel stupid. When they describe the action on audio they see things I'm not seeing on video, like where the puck is going on the ice—places like "the slot" and "the point," which are not marked on the ice, although "the crease" is, and they're not talking about pressed breezers, which I thought for a long time, and when I found out the hard way—by asking—what it really was, I felt stupid.

There are certain things I understand about hockey, but then everybody understands them because how could you miss them? Like "charging." Your kid (your kid is why you see all this hockey in the first place) goes on the road for a weekend series and you have to stay in a hotel for two nights and you pull out your Master Card and put the weekend on it, that's charging, and when I do it I feel stupid.

Sometimes as I watch the frustration the hockey players experience in chasing that little black puck around a slippery surface while being knocked around by other people just for trying to achieve a goal, I think of hockey as a metaphor for life, because the same things happen to you when you try to accomplish anything—there's always somebody in your way to knock you off balance and stop you from reaching your goal—and when my mind wanders down those philosophical pathways I miss something on the ice like "hooking" or "slashing" and I ask somebody what happened and when they tell me I feel stupid.

Originally appeared in the Duluth News-Tribune *on Sunday, February 26, 1989.*

PART II:

OUTRAGEOUS NONSENSE

OUTRAGEOUS NONSENSE

Before I began assembling this collection, I thought there would be a lot more columns that could only be regarded as outrageous nonsense than there were. Turns out there were plenty, but plenty of others, too; even some serious columns found in other chapters.

But this chapter truly represents my penchant for writing outrageous nonsense, including one of many columns about my fictitious wife "Blanche." Fictitious is right, since Blanche bore no resemblance to my actual wife, to whom this book is dedicated. But Blanche columns were popular in their time, and, surprisingly (at least to me), many readers were led to believe I was describing my own domestic situation. Nonsense. Outrageous nonsense.

Other examples of outrageous nonsense in this chapter were plucked from perhaps 10 times that many in the files. I just liked these; many made me laugh as I was writing, and I hoped others would find them funny, too.

A column called "The Cheaps" is included to document once and for all a phenomenon of the 1950s that I believe started in my high school, Duluth Denfeld, but spread to other local schools during that period. The column explains what "cheaps" are, and most readers will recognize the feeling right away, even if they don't call it that. I'm happy to say that the cheaps had a brief revival in the late 1980s and early 1990s at Duluth East High School, when my own two children contaminated their friends with the cheaps, and all were forever infected.

From being the only male at the movie *Little Women* to riding down the elevator in Duluth's tallest office building with a toilet to being confronted with nothing but salmon specials at a restaurant, most outrageously nonsensical columns were drawn from real experiences. They follow.

This Ain't the "Little Women" This Guy's Used To

OK, I admit it. I went to the movie, *Little Women*. How was I supposed to know no men would be there? I saw one other guy. We shook hands as we left the theater.

So what's it like being a man at *Little Women*? At first you don't notice. Waiting for it to start, you sit there chewin' your tobacco and spittin' on the floor just like normal. Then, as the theater starts to fill up, you realize you are surrounded by women and you begin to wonder, "Hey, is there something wrong with me?" Or, "Hey, are these women going to *think* there's something wrong with me?"

It ain't easy being a man at a woman's movie. Heck, I had good intentions. I always favored little women—you know, in *Playboy*, and stuff like that. The petite ones. Some guys like big German women, but not me. Little women—that's my style.

So along comes this movie and I see the ads in the paper. It's the holidays and I ain't been doin' much but sittin' around drinkin' beer, watchin' football and dreamin' about when one of those monster pickup truck shows comes back to town.

They got these pickup trucks with huge wheels on 'em and they go around crushin' Detroit irons like they was little ants or somethin'.

But anyways, back to when I was the only man, almost, at this *Little Women.* The Vikes were still in the running, so was Green Bay, but I had a night off of watchin' football on the tube so I decided to read.

You seen that Whitney's catalog of car parts and the gadgets? I get it in the mail. They got accessories in there you wouldn't never dream were available that cheap.

Anyways, I'm readin' the Whitney catalog and then I picks up the newspaper and see the movie ads. *IQ* is one of the movies showing, and I'm tempted because of my being so smart and all, but when I see *Little Women* my eyes just about pop out of my head. I remember this little number in *Penthouse*, oh, I'd say it was 1978…well, I get carried away.

Trouble is, I can't leave my "little woman" home and run off to this movie alone, so I says, "Listen, Dollface, why'n't the two of us take in a show tonight or sumpin' like that."

Well, she's been cleaning up all the decorations after the holidays like a good housewife and was happy I asked because I hadn't taken her to a show in maybe a decade or two. Who keeps track? So she asks me what show, and I kind of casually say, "Oh, I don't know, there's this one called *Little Women,* might be kinda interestin'."

Well she acts real surprised like. "You want to go to *Little Women?*" she says.

I didn't want to act too eager. "Wouldn't mind. I think they're kinda cute."

Well, I gotta bring this here little essay to a close pretty quick now, but I knew somethin' must be eradically wrong when I turn up as one of the only men in the theater with all these college-looking women givin' me looks like I'm some kind of freak. Never did any guy want to be some-wheres else, like maybe at a neighborhood bar, more than me.

Just let me say that I know now this was some so-called classic 100-year-old women's story that every schoolgirl read when us guys was out in the garage puttin' dual exhausts, twin carbs, full-race cams and Offy heads on our cars. I mean, there ain't an ankle showing in this entire flick. These were not the little women I remembered from *Playboy*, like that time they had "Little Women of Rutgers." I saved that one.

I shudda went to *IQ*. That's more my speed. They got Einstein in there.

Originally appeared in the Duluth News-Tribune *on Wednesday, January 11, 1995.*

The Cheaps

I'm coming to a crossroads of my life this week and I feel I ought to do a column about it. No self-respecting columnist would pass up the chance to pause and reflect when such a milestone is reached.

When I see others do it though, it gives me the cheaps, so naturally I hesitate somewhat.

The cheaps? You ask.

Yes, the cheaps. During one period of my life, everybody I knew instantly recognized what "the cheaps" meant, but I've found out lately that most people I come in contact with don't know the expression.

The cheaps meant "feel cheap" or "slightly embarrassed," sometimes for someone else, sometimes for you. They fall somewhere between a blush and hot ears.

But of course, you'd have to be in the neighborhood of 40 to understand that. And that's the milestone I'm reaching this week. I've been in the neighborhood of 40 for quite a while now, and for the past year she's been living next door. On Thursday, like it or not, she moves in.

So here I am, on the threshold of 40, and as I pause, reflect and look back over the years, well—what can I say—I get the cheaps.

The cheaps and I are very old friends. I've spent at least two decades of the four I've now chalked up feeling them and, despite my advancing years, there's no letup. It seems like almost any situation in life that requires an emotional reaction, however light, I get the cheaps. Let me cite a few examples:

I get them when singers get up to sing. I get them when speakers get up to speak. I get them when somebody tells me a joke I've already heard. I get them when I catch the eye of another driver stopped alongside me at a red light.

I get them when I dance or watch others dance. I get them when I'm supposed to sing in a group, like everyone doing "The Star Spangled Banner" before a performance or game. I get them when I have to eat alone in a restaurant. When I was young, single and dating, I got them when I delivered my date to her door after getting them when I picked her up. I get them in wedding reception lines.

I get national and historical cheaps too. I get them when Johnny Carson interviews people in the audience. I get them when George Washington crosses the Delaware or when anybody recites the Gettysburg Address. I get them when Richard Nixon walks, when Jimmy Carter smiles, when Danny Thomas materializes or when The Pips back Gladys Knight. I get them when Woody Allen says Mozart's *Jupiter Symphony* is one of the things that makes life worth living, and when Carl Sagan talks about life on other planets.

Local and area cheaps? They abound. Reverence toward the Boundary Waters Canoe Area gives me the cheaps. UMD hockey fanaticism invokes them, as does Viking Fever. Jogging gives me the cheaps. I get the cheaps asking the price of anything.

The cheaps used to bother me when I was younger. In other words, I got the cheaps about having the cheaps. But not anymore. I've come to regard them as an old friend, and as I embark on my fifth decade, instead of trying to overcome them I'm going to embrace them. (Any kind of embrace gives me the cheaps.)

It seems to me that once you reach what they call mid-life (that word gives me the cheaps), you ought to be able to have the cheaps as often as you damn-well please (swearing in public gives me the cheaps) as long as you've taken the trouble to cultivate them.

So if you see me on the street, or meet me at a movie, or greet me at a garage, or buss me on a bus or regale me in a restaurant (alliteration gives me the cheaps), the chances are I'll have the cheaps, or, if not, they're just around the corner.

It's been a long time since I've written a serious column like this and, to tell you the truth, I've got the cheaps about it.

Originally appeared in the Duluth News-Tribune *on Sunday, September 30, 1979.*

DOES ELVIS LOOK LIKE THE STATUE OF LIBERTY?

*T*he other night as I sat dozing in the living room before the television set, as I do whenever I watch TV, I was awakened by the stirring sounds of "America the Beautiful."

And there, on the screen, in semi-profile, close in, was the face of Elvis Presley. As the music swelled, the camera backed away from its subject and—I couldn't believe my eyes—it was the Statue of Liberty.

"Of course," I said. "That's it. Elvis Presley looks like the Statue of Liberty."

My wife was sitting nearby. "Are you nuts?" she asked delicately.

"Take a good look; look at the brow, the nose and the mouth," I said. "They're all Elvis Presley."

But by the time she was able to focus on the statue, the camera, obviously on a helicopter, had backed too far away. The picture showed the whole statue, torch and all.

The discovery actually resolved a gnawing feeling I've had for years whenever I saw a picture of Elvis or tuned into one of his movies on TV for about five minutes—which is about all anybody can take of an Elvis Presley movie. Whenever I saw Elvis's image, it triggered some kind of comparison in my mind, but I couldn't place it until the other night when I realized he looks exactly like the Statue of Liberty—through the face.

Take away the crown, take away Lady Liberty's hairdo, take away the spit curls in front of the statue's ears, and concentrate on the principal parts of the face, especially the mouth, and it's Elvis. I'm talking about the early Elvis, before he put on a lot of extra weight and became puffy-looking.

There are those who might resent my saying that Elvis looks like the Statue of Liberty, rather than saying that the statue looks like Elvis, which is also the case. And there are those who would resent any comparison at all, with some believing it is an insult to the statue, and others insisting it is an insult to Elvis. Good for them.

I happen to think that Elvis would be proud to be compared to the Statue of Liberty, which is easy for me to say, and a hard fact to check.

All of this is a matter of no importance, of course, in light of rising federal deficits and trouble in the war-torn Middle East, not to mention El Salvador and Nicaragua, but I found out the next day that comparing Elvis and the Statue of Liberty can arouse more passion in people than the major issues of the presidential campaign.

Checking around the office to see if anyone else had noticed the resemblance, several people reacted as though I were being sacrilegious. Others reacted as though I were blind.

But a few others had to admit I had a point there.

What do you say? If you agree that Elvis Presley looks like the Statue of Liberty, go to your toilet and flush it at exactly 9:45 tonight and we'll check with the water and gas department to see if it showed up on their monitors. If you don't think Elvis looks like the Statue of Liberty, do nothing, unless, of course, you absolutely have to at 9:45 in which case you will be counted with those who agree.

That method of polling is not precise, mind you, but it's definitely in the spirit of these ruminations. And it's cheap, too.

Originally appeared in the Duluth News-Tribune & Herald *on Wednesday, September 26, 1984.*

BLANCHE: CONSTITUTIONAL QUESTIONS

*L*eafing through one of Blanche's bowling magazines recently, I came across an advertisement for terrycloth towels inscribed with the "Bowler's Prayer."

Dear Lord, the prayer goes, *I have but one request and I shall not ask for more; that I, before I'm laid to rest, might bowl a perfect score.*

It struck me as somehow inappropriate and possibly illegal; in violation of separation of church and bowling as guaranteed by, if not the U.S. Constitution, certainly the Bowlers' Constitution.

Blanche felt differently about it. "I see nothing wrong with prayer in the bowling alley," she said when I voiced my concern.

"Nor do I, Blanche," I said assertively, "bowlers can pray silently all they want. The question is, should there be a prescribed prayer all written out for them? I doubt the Supreme Court would allow it."

"The President is for prayer in the bowling alleys," Blanche retorted, flushing slightly in anger but maintaining control. "Now quit worrying about things that are above you and get busy on your spring housecleaning."

Blanche has a way of dismissing things by putting me to work on my homemaking chores, which she hasn't got time for because she's too busy watching soap operas on TV and serving as chaplain of her bowling team.

Not that Blanche is that religious, mind you. She's no pillar of the church, but she does watch TV preachers like Jimmy Swaggart to guide her in her bowling team chaplaincy chores. She feels a kinship with Swaggart because he is a cousin to Jerry Lee Lewis, the unholy rock 'n' roller.

But I was in no mood to be dismissed when Blanche and I were discussing separation of church and bowling, so I persisted.

"What would happen if you were reciting the Bowler's Prayer at the bowling alley and someone in the next lane objected?" I postulated.

Blanche pondered that one for a moment, taking time to light a Virginia Slim with her rhinestone-encrusted Bic as she leaned back in her Lay-Z-Girl reclining rocker and swept taco chip crumbs from her yellow muu-muu. "Let them bowl in the Soviet Union," she finally belched. "You can bet they have separation of church and bowling over there."

This was a side of Blanche that even I hadn't seen—a sort of meditative, patriotic, devotional side that belied her usual devil-couldn't-care-less demeanor. It could have something to do with her recent weight loss of two pounds in three months, bringing her muu-muu size down to 22. She's rightfully proud of the achievement, which she accomplished with the help of a newspaper diet plan that could have her down to a size 18 in four years.

It wasn't long after our conversation on the subject that Blanche and I were unexpectedly invited by Blanche's half brother, Whit, to a National Rifle Association forum/banquet—a fancy affair held in a hotel ballroom. The topic for the evening was, "Practical Applications of Armor-Piercing Bullets."

And much to her surprise, Blanche was called upon to give the invocation, possibly because she was wearing a black muu-muu and the leader of the meeting mistook her for a holy woman. Unable to decline, a flustered Blanche stood and bowed her head. "Dear Lord," she said, "I have but one request and I shall not ask for more; that I, before I'm laid to rest, might bowl a perfect score."

The prayer got a big hand, and then we all sang "The Star Spangled Banner."

Originally appeared in the Duluth News Tribune & Herald *on Sunday, March 25, 1984.*

Baboons Cruelly Being Forced to Write Assembly Instructions

Well, I finally replaced my 23-year-old rotary power lawnmower with a new one just like it (only not as good). It is a sign of aging when you hear yourself saying, "Yup, they don't make things as good as they used to," but they don't.

Not that the old mower doesn't start anymore. It just doesn't cut anymore. So I bought a new one, choosing a model not for its reputation, not for its versatility (like "mulching" and grass-catcher bags), but on the basis of how cheap it was pricewise.

The new lawnmower came in a box maybe three feet square and two feet deep, which was my first hint it had to be assembled ("put together"). This is an immediate red flag for me because I am not good at putting things together—are you? Questioning a sales clerk on the difficulty, he responded, "It's easy—won't take you half an hour. Just attach the handle, hook up the controls and start mowing."

"Uh, huh."

So I took it home. But I didn't assemble it right away. I left it in the garage for a few days to give myself time to mentally prepare for putting it together. Whenever I've put things together in the past, I've had important questions about the "instructions."

The instructions are always unintelligible because they are not written by humans who know how to explain things in writing, but by baboons. Zoos nationally are raising funds by having their baboons moonlight writing instructions for things that have to be put together. Only a few insiders like me know this because they're covering it up. ("They" are the Council on Foreign Relations and the Tri-Lateral Commission.)

But the hapless baboons only work for somebody else anyway. Shouldn't that person be responsible? Yes. Aren't the CEOs of the lawnmower companies responsible for what their firms are doing to the public?

Why certainly. Years ago I was almost driven over the edge attempting to put a 10-speed bicycle together for my daughter. But for the grace of God, I would have ended up a ward of the state in one of its diminishing number of regional treatment centers (formerly "loony bins").

A few nights before I attempted to put the new rotary power lawnmower together, I had a wonderful dream. I dreamed I stalked the CEO of the company that manufactured it (he was only eight hours away by car in suburban Chicago), captured him, tied him up and brought him to my garage where I would be assembling the lawnmower in my underwear. (Of course in my underwear—it was a dream.)

In the garage, I hung him from a hook normally used to suspend bicycles from the rafters—not by the neck, of course, but by the ropes around his chest area so he could answer questions as I assembled.

Even with the CEO hanging around, assembling the lawnmower took a good four hours. The reason was that the instructions identified various parts by their professional engineering nomenclature. The words "bolt" and "nut" to describe nuts and bolts are unknown to the instruction writers. They think ordinary people know what a "Knobloch brace" is.

Example: "Place Knobloch brace on the right side of rear housing when facing front or left side of front housing when facing north."

"Why do they do that?" I queried the CEO of my dream, who was twisting in the wind like a Clinton appointee.

"Let me bring in my management team and get back to you," said the CEO.

That was not satisfactory, so I began heating a branding iron in the hot coals I had started.

I continued: "It says here, 'Place the vertrit clamp directly beneath the bowtung and tighten with a smolvar hex. Beware, over tightening could cause meltdown.' Just what does that mean?"

The CEO looked down from his perch and pleaded, "I've got a wife and kids, a mother, a home, a dog, a station wagon. Have mercy."

I laughed a long, crazy laugh. "You should have thought of that before you got into the instruction business," I drooled—reaching for the red-hot branding iron shaped in the initials CEO.

"Wake up! Wake up! You're having a terrible nightmare!" It was my orderly.

"No, I'm not," I smiled.

Originally appeared in the Duluth News-Tribune *on Sunday, June 13, 1993.*

ART FOR ART'S SAKE

On the wall of my living room is a painting many people who don't know anything about art would call "abstract" or "modern" or "hideous."

I don't know much about art either, but I know what I like. I like this painting. It's got all kinds of goofy geometric shapes and wavy lines, mostly in black, on a beige field. One circle topped by a triangle suggests a schoolroom dunce, and what looks like a drop of water makes it look like the dunce is suffering from a drippy cold. Makes me think of my own school days.

In one corner is a shape that resembles a coat hanger, and in the middle of everything is a simple, ragged X. Somewhere in this hodgepodge is a smattering of orange. The painting has a discreet black frame and is nicely matted.

Sometimes when I'm relaxing in the living room I sit and stare at the painting and it talks to me in its own quiet way. Not out loud, mind you. But art has its own way of speaking, asking questions that are not always easy to answer—but are important questions to ask. Questions like, "Thirsty?"

I get the feeling visitors to my home do not like this painting. I think they think it is a monstrosity, a denial of their artistic values, a travesty, a sacrilege, and that we are nuts to have such a conglomeration of circles and triangles and wavy lines on our living room wall. Many wouldn't pay a dollar for it at a rummage sale. I don't care.

Why all this now?

A week or so ago the paper carried a story about a touring exhibit, called "The People's Choice," currently at the Landmark Center in St. Paul. It features paintings prepared by asking people what they like to see in paintings, and what they don't like to see. This was done by having them fill out questionnaires listing their preferences in theme and color.

The results showed the favorite color is blue and people prefer "representational" (true to life) paintings of outdoor scenes with wild animals and people at leisure. The painting in this touring exhibit representing the United States shows a mountain lake with trees in the foreground, two deer near the shore, a hippopotamus, a few modern-looking people strolling along and George Washington standing nobly nearby.

Visiting shopping mall galleries, I would have thought ducks at sunrise would have been included. And where's Elvis?

The artists also discussed what kind of paintings Americans hate the most. Let me quote from the story: "…randomly scattered, overlapping triangles and rectangles in shades of gold, orange, peach and teal."

Sound familiar?

It did to me. I've got it in my living room. A dunce with a drippy cold looking at a crooked coat hanger and the hint of an upcoming game of tick-tack-toe.

Now I know what it feels like to be in a minority. It feels good.

Originally appeared in the Duluth News-Tribune *on Sunday, November 21, 1999.*

THE HERALD ANGELS CROON

*S*everal holiday seasons ago I wrote a column against "Rudolph the Red-Nosed Reindeer," causing a public outcry that still sinks me into the depths of Christmas depression. Well, maybe not depression, but recession. Actually, perhaps not recession either, but certainly downturn.

My thesis was that Rudolph, as a Christmas carol (the column was not against Rudolph as a reindeer but rather as a song), was a reindeer-come-lately number that wasn't even around when I was a child and learned my important Christmas carols, such as "Jingle Bells," "Up on the Rooftop Click-Click-Click, Down Through the Chimney With Ol' St. Nick," and "Jolly Old St. Nicholas, Lend Me Your Ears" (or something like that).

Therefore, I have never accepted "Rudolph the Red-Nosed Reindeer" as a bona fide Christmas song or included it on my Christmas music listening list.

Each holiday season I try to add to my collection of Christmas recordings, now mostly CDs. Last weekend I went in search of a new Christmas CD but failed to find one that seemed appropriate.

Some of the hip-hop stars are starting to produce Christmas albums, but I lean more toward "Christmas With the Philadelphia Orchestra Featuring Singers From the Metropolitan Opera and the Mormon Tabernacle Choir"-type albums, so there is a gulf there that can't be bridged. I looked at a CD called "Christmas on Death Row" (honest, this album exists; who would make that up?), but I was already a little depressed—make that recessed. Well, maybe downturned.

But on Thursday morning in the shower, I was thinking about Rudolph and his red nose and the ridicule he goes through every year at this time, and I began to wonder (as I hurriedly washed my feet) if the song shouldn't be eliminated from the Christmas roster entirely in these politically correct times.

Should we be openly stating he is a "red-nosed reindeer" with a "very shiny nose" that, you might even say, "glows"? What kind of talk is that: pointing out physical characteristics that by almost every measure—outside of traffic signal circles—are considered to be unattractive?

Then we tell the world that all of the other reindeer laughed and called him names and wouldn't let "poor" Rudolph "join in any reindeer games." If that isn't condoning bully-like behavior, I don't know what is.

Even Santa Claus gets into the act, saying, "Rudolph, with your nose so bright." Thanks a lot, Jolly Old Elf; how'd you like it if somebody said, "Santa, with your belly so full of jelly"?

See what I mean? This is a very bad number for our children to learn. We could be raising insensitive bullies intolerant of those who are a little different.

Sure, Rudolph is a hero in the end, but isn't that a little late? If I were Rudolph, I wouldn't guide the sleigh on that foggy Christmas Eve. I'd throw down my badge and leave the North Pole.

Speaking of Christmas carols, the newspaper reported last week that President Bush clearly didn't know the words to "Hark! The Herald Angels Sing" at a recent gala holiday concert on television.

What a colossal gaffe. Everybody knows that the carol goes, "Hark the *Herald* angels croon, / Glory to the *News Tribune*."

Don't they?

Originally appeared in the Duluth News Tribune *on Sunday, December 16, 2001.*

HELP STAMP OUT PLAGIARISM

*O*h, woe! Oh, lamentation. The specter of plagiarism has once again cast its ominous shadow across our favored land. I deplore plagiarism. Plagiarism is the second-to-last refuge of a scoundrel. Plagiarism is the scourge of mankind. You can always count on a plagiarist for fancy prose style. Poetry, too. That said....

"Now listen, my children, and you shall hear, of the midnight ride of Paul Revere...throw off the covers, tear off the sheets, for the 50-yard dash to the toilet seat."

That's an old Boy Scout poem I made up. I've made up lots of stuff like: "There are strange things done in the midnight sun, by the men who moil for gold; and the Arctic trails have their secret tales, that would make your blood run cold..." Eat your heart out John Beargrease.

I'm a veritable font of originality. A cornucopia of verbiage, and also nouniage, adjectiviage, adverbiage and conjunctivitis.

That's my business, kid. James is the name, writing's the game. Try this little sendup: "I know not what course others may take; but as for me, give me liberty, or give me death."

Has the ring of revolution to it, don'tcha think? I should publish. How about this: "This vehicle stops at all railroad crossings." Mine, all mine. They're painting it on school buses now. Proud? Only as a peacock.

"It came upon a midnight clearly, on the shores of Gitchee Gumee, while I pondered weak and weary, by the shining Big-Sea-Water; asked the Raven: 'What's the mattah, who's that clown there, the mad hattah?' Quoth the raven, 'Nevermore.'"

But I continue. "Not to go back is somewhat to advance, and men must walk, at least, before they dance." Women, too. Takes two to tango or do the fandango. "Frankly, my dear, I could have danced all night, and still have asked for more."

"When in the course of Human Events…" I know not what course others took, but I didn't take Human Events as one of my courses in school, did you? "But I was desolate and sick of an old passion. I have been faithful to thee, Cynara! in my fashion."

Ho, hum. Just spills out of me like the milk moustache of human kindness. Did I say milk? "Water, water everywhere, and all the boards did shrink; water, water everywhere, nor any drop to drink." Fear not. "Virtue, though in rags, will keep me warm."

The most recent plagiarism scandal involves a couple of my favorite historians whose works I explore from time to time when I get a chance to read, perchance to sleep. "Toupee or not toupee? That is the question." Here's another: "Do I dare to eat a peach, wear white pants and walk along the beach?"

"Presume not God to scan, the proper study of mankind is man." Oh sure, and "go and catch a falling star, get with child a mandrake root." Put that in your pipe and smoke it, although "now laughing friends deride, tears I cannot hide, when a lovely flame dies, smoke gets in your…" lungs.

Heck, folks, "poems are made by fools like me, but only God can make a tree...." "And I admit the general rule, that every poet is a fool, but you yourself may serve to show it, that every fool is not a poet."

Final note: This original material comes by way of my imagination. Any similarity to passages published elsewhere through the ages is purely unmistakable. Like all plagiarists, I apologize.

Originally appeared in the Duluth News Tribune *on Sunday, February 3, 2002.*

DOUBLE BUBBLE, TOILET TROUBLE

So I'm on an elevator, descending from the uppermost floor of Duluth's tallest office building, the Alworth. I'm alone when I start the descent.

But a few floors down—three, perhaps—the elevator comes to a halt, the doors slide open and there, waiting to get on, is a...toilet.

A toilet is all I can see from where I'm standing. It is disconnected from its pipes and on a small cart, accompanied by a building maintenance worker who comes into view as he pushes the toilet onto the elevator with me.

Double bubble, toilet trouble, I'm thinking. I have to say something. "Well, this is certainly a first for me—riding an elevator with a toilet," I said.

"It's not a first for me," grumbles the maintenance man.

"This royal throne of kings, this scepter'd isle, this earth of majesty, this seat of Mars..." declaims the toilet, quoting Shakespeare. Well, no, the toilet didn't exactly say that. I was thinking that's what it would say if it could talk.

I did acknowledge to the maintenance worker that, yup, I suppose you do ride elevators with toilets all the time, an experience in life that I am not disappointed I missed. It's at surrealistic times like this when you would welcome Salvador Dali.

The elevator continues to descend. A few more floors down it comes to a halt again and a man gets on, joining me, the maintenance worker and the toilet. It is not Salvador Dali, who is dead but whose moustache inspired the discoverers of Viagra.

The new passenger observes the situation, but seems nonplused—like he rides elevators with toilets all the time. I begin to think that I have missed an experience everyone else has had.

"Well," I say to the man who gets on, "what do you think of this—riding down the elevator with a toilet?"

He clearly wasn't planning to engage in conversation, but, when asked a direct question, he couldn't ignore it. He mutters something forgettable because I have forgotten it. Nothing more is said. I alight from the elevator in the lobby, leaving the toilet behind.

Thinking about it later, though, the experience reminded me of what a jerk I can be at times. I've got to learn to do better. Any normal person would have welcomed the toilet with open arms and not tried to make a big deal about it. Toilets are natural things, a part of everyone's life every day of their lives unless they have a cabin with an outhouse, or camp in the BWCA (which stands for Bad Water Closet Accommodations).

Surely you'd expect a toilet could get on an elevator without some smart-mouth making stupid remarks. Can't you push a toilet through an office building anymore in America without facing ridicule or wisecracks? And can't a person get on the elevator with the toilet and be left alone?

Who's this grinning fool bothering everybody on the elevator, anyway? Just ride it out and get on with your life, like any normal person.

And worse, you go back to your newspaper and write a column about it that potentially could be seen by 200,000 people, not counting the Internet? Get a life, man!

I've decided I am the trouble with America today.

Originally appeared in the Duluth News Tribune *on Sunday, May 5, 2002.*

A LOOK AT WHO'S WHO IN THE FAMILY

I got a telephone call the other day from my first cousin once removed, now living in Arizona.

"Well, hello, first cousin once removed, how are you?" I responded when he identified himself.

I suppose he was surprised that I suddenly knew exactly what our relationship is. We had always just regarded ourselves as cousins, knowing we weren't first cousins because his grandmother was my aunt. Maybe we thought we were second cousins.

But I like to be precise. Also, recently on public radio I heard an explanation of just who is what in cousin relationships. In keeping with this column's public service obligations, today I share this information with readers so that if they win the lottery and their first cousins once removed—or second cousins—come calling, they'll know who not to give money to.

For a subject so complex, I believe it is best to use the question and answer (Q and A) format often employed by police when grilling suspects schooled in genealogy. So here we go:

Q: Where were you when the bank was robbed?

A: I was visiting my second cousin in jail.

Q: How do you know he's your second cousin?

A: Because my father and his mother were first cousins.

Q: How do you know he isn't your first cousin once removed?

A: If he were my first cousin once removed, his grandmother would be my aunt.

Q: Don't get smart with me, tough guy. Do you have a first cousin once removed, and if so where was he when you robbed the bank?

A: I've got a first cousin who was once removed from a hockey game for high sticking.

Q: What is the difference between a second cousin and a first cousin once removed, anyway?

A: Your first cousin's son or daughter is your first cousin once removed. That person is your son or daughter's second cousin and vice versa.

Q: What if you don't have children?

A: They don't have any second cousins.

Q: What if your first cousin doesn't have children?

A: You don't have any first cousins once removed.

Q: What are you to your first cousin once removed's children's children.

A: They are either your first cousin twice removed, your second cousin once removed or your third cousin.

Q: Can first cousins once removed marry?

A: Not me and my first cousin once removed: We're both already married and both males.

Q: What does being both males have to do with it these days?

A: Oops. Forgot.

Q: Is Saddam Hussein's first cousin once removed a threat to the United States?

A: "Once removed" has an entirely different meaning in Iraq. Saddam Hussein has removed all of his cousins.

Q: My mother-in-law's first cousin once removed came to my wedding and ate like a horse and drank like a fish but did not send a gift. What is my mother-in-law's first cousin once removed to me?

A: A glutton, a lush and cheap.

There you have it. For further information on this subject, do not contact me. I'm thoroughly confused.

Originally appeared in the Duluth News Tribune *on Sunday, October 13, 2002.*

Here Comes a Plethora of Salmon

*I*t has come to my undivided attention that a trend might be developing in our community that could lead to an alarming use of "big" words that only college professors understand.

As his supporters and adversaries alike know, President George W. Bush is a man of "little" words, and he often gets all tangled up when his writers insert big words in the text of his pronouncements. Oh sorry... "pronouncements" is kind of big. Should have said his "speeches," which isn't exactly the same thing but close enough.

Shouldn't we be following our leader?

We here at the newspaper are at fault, too. Newspapers are supposed to be written for sixth-graders, but with declining enrollment in the schools, we've got to reach out by sticking in some bigger words now and then to attract seventh-graders, maybe even a few in eighth grade. Not antidisestablishmentarianism, mind you (we're not up to St. Scholastica

standards yet), but certainly an occasional supercalifragilisticexpialido-
cious wouldn't hurt.

Why all this now? Ordering lunch the other day at a well-known
Duluth restaurant, the server listed the day's specials:

"Today's specials are a salmon BLT, salmon salad, salmon fillet,
salmon soup..." she recited, then continued as an aside, "...we've got a
plethora of salmon today."

Well, well. I'll say that's a plethora of salmon.

Many fine, upstanding, loyal—even patriotic—Americans might
not actually be that familiar with the term "plethora" though, so (I hope
not condescendingly) I will point out that it means "lots of" or "too
much." Too much of anything. Like salmon. Even a little salmon is
too much salmon as far as I'm concerned. At least the restaurant wasn't
featuring salmon loaf, a dish served in my growing-up home so reviled
by the children that we were forced to flee to a nearby park just to avoid
the smell.

Of course the restaurant's salmon specials didn't include Salmon
Rushdie, Salmon P. Chase or Jack Salmon, but, all things considered, I
think we could call it a plethora.

Still, not every waitperson speaks of plethoras in the kitchen—not
that the word is *that* big—but it illustrates the big-word problem and
also brings up another danger we've got to start watching out for before it
spreads to Hermantown and beyond: The caliber of waitpersons might be
rising at an alarming rate.

Only rudimentary—make that "limited"—applied research shows
that many men and women taking jobs as restaurant servers have attended
or are going to *college*.

In other words, there is a paucity (shortage) of the old barfly-type
servers (not to be sexist, but they were women) who kept the strong American tradition of the double negative alive for so long. "You don't got no
money, you don't get no boilermaker, Slicko." Boilermaker is a longish
word itself, but most people understand it as "a shot and a snit," followed
quickly by another shot and snit. Fifteen minutes later you're preserving

the tradition of the double negative in America yourself, and probably taking up smoking again to boot.

But enough alarming news. Here's some sunshine: We've all heard of a gaggle of geese, a pride of lions, a warren of rabbits, a school of fish, a brace of kinsmen, a coven of witches.

Our articulate salmon server might have given the world a new description for a whole bunch of salmon: "A plethora of salmon." It has a ring to it, don't you think?

Originally appeared in the Duluth News Tribune *on Sunday, March 6, 2005.*

PART III:

SLICES OF LIFE

SLICES OF LIFE

Don't look for too many laughs in this chapter, which is mainly devoted to columns inspired by the passages in family life, from early parenting ("Call of the Child") right through to "Confessions of a New Grandfather."

"Call of the Child" is another bit of doggerel posing as a poem penned when the children were young (but not infants) and invariably made a certain announcement involving nature's call immediately upon embarking on a family car trip. Who hasn't experienced that?

This section also includes thoughts on having your kids graduate from high school and the loss of a beloved dog that I hope reflect readers' own emotions at such times. And that most important family event—a wedding—("Father of the Groom") allowed me to revisit the alarming rise of hugging in America as a way of greeting people—even relative strangers (and certainly strange relatives). It's a theme that has appeared several times over the years in my columns, to the point where some family and friends are not sure if they should hug me at all. Good.

I was quite surprised while assembling this collection that there were so many "serious" columns to choose from, since I thought of myself mainly as a humor columnist. But there are times when events are so compelling they simply cannot be ignored. An account of one such time will be found in "The Boys Who Went Too Far on the Bus" in this chapter. It speaks for itself, but readers might be interested to learn that the boys involved were identified after that column ran, and dealt with appropriately. One can only hope they survived their adolescence.

So here are some of life's passages filtered through the eyes and thoughts of one man, husband, father, grandfather, newspaperman (a.k.a journalist) and citizen.

CALL OF THE CHILD

I wish I had an answer
To a question I've long had:
It's why my kids and others,
Can drive you raving mad,
Whenever we're away from home,
And where there is no can,
It's then that they feel nature's call,
Despite your best laid plan.

You can steer them to a toilet
Just before you go somewhere;
You can dip their feet in water,
You can pat them on their hair,
You can plead and you can holler,
You can tell them that they should,
You can demonstrate the process,
But it won't do any good.

'Cause as soon as you get started,
With your destination set;
You're in the car three miles from home,
The engine's not warm yet,
You get the word from the back seat,
They tell you loud and clear,
"Hey Dad (or Mom) I've got to go,"
You needn't ask them where.

Now here's the part that gets me,
And I know I'm not alone,
It's a question that I ponder,
It's a thing that I bemoan:
Why can't they do their business
Before the journey starts?
Why do they always have to
Put the horse behind the cart?

So you put the question to them,
And the answer stays the same,
It's as sure as death and taxes,
It's as positive as rain;
"You've had a chance to go before,
Would it have done such harm
To let us make some miles,
Before you sound an alarm?"

But the answer never varies,
It's as though they're in cahoots.
They never fail to give it—
It goes way back to their roots;
You don't really have to listen,
When they give the reason why.
"I didn't need to go then,
So I didn't even try."

"I didn't need to go then,"
And you know that it is a fact,
It's the way the kids all operate
Their urinary tracts.
It's as though their little bladders
Are timed with a device,
To only sound a warning when
The time is far from right.

"I didn't need to go then,"
It resounds down through the ages,
From the time of Tutankhamen,
Through the days of saints and sages,
It was heard by old King Henry
When Elizabeth was young,
It was told to Sigmund Freud,
It was heard by Carl Jung.

When'er the time is rotten,
Such as when you're in a church,
A little voice will whimper
That it's in a painful lurch.
And the hushed voice of the parent,
As they're headed for the door,
Begs the eternal question,
"Why didn't you go before?"

And like something out of scripture,
The needful child will vow,
"I didn't have to go then.
But I sure do need to now."
So the little hand is taken,
And led to you know where,
With the parent's resignation,
Reflected in his stare.

Still it's with full recognition,
As I write out this complaint,
That in another year or two
The kids will show restraint.
Then I know I'll come to cherish,
The days of the same old story:
When we trod the low and trespassed routes,
To all those lavatories.

Originally appeared in the Duluth News-Tribune *on Sunday, February 3, 1980.*

FATHER'S DAY

I don't think I'll ever get used to being the father on Father's Day. That day, it seems to me, is set aside to revere one's own parent, and not to be revered by one's children.

But like every other dad, I suppose I'll have to go along with the gag on what has to be one of the two or three most ridiculous quasi-holiday observations of the year.

And while it undoubtedly keeps the cash registers ringing, a day set aside to "honor" fathers nationwide seems a bit misguided. For it is my opinion that to be a father is an honor, something that should be revered for its own sake—daily.

Children seldom realize it while they are still properly referred to as children, but to most of their fathers they represent his contribution to the hope of the future.

While they are shopping for a tie or a new sweater or golf club to give dad on national Father's Day, they don't realize, at least while they are young, that they already have given him the most precious gift ever presented—themselves.

They have given him an opportunity to importantly influence the life of another; to guide it in the directions he deems important; to protect it from what he sees as the dangers, both physical and emotional, without blindly turning their backs on all evil so they won't recognize it when it comes up and slaps them in the face some day.

And the children don't realize that they have given him his most important reason for acting responsibly in all facets of living, for he knows they are depending on him.

The children also give their dads the opportunity to re-live their own childhood days and to pass on some of the things that were important to him when he was their age, whether it be how to swing a Louisville slugger or a favorite bedtime story.

There are a lot of other little things, too, that taken in sum become more important than one realizes. Children give their dads (and their mothers, too, but this is Father's Day) an excuse to go to Walt Disney movies, or visit a zoo or go to a carnival or a parade.

They drag their parents through museums, to concerts and to school plays and expose them to any number of ideas that might never have occurred to them, sitting comfortably a solid generation ahead of what youth is thinking.

What kind of blind idealist wouldn't admit that being a parent can have its headaches, too, and that a lot of them are caused by the children? But as every adult knows, and the children are going to find out some day, *not* being a parent probably has just as many headaches so you might as well go ahead and have the kids.

Every father knows, of course, that about the time his children are able to grasp all of these things, they're going to leave him and start the cycle all over again. And he knows he's going to smilingly accept that fact of life even though it might hurt him a little to see it happen.

Then he'll graciously receive the tie or a new sweater or golf club on Father's Day knowing full well that the gifts themselves mean nothing on that day compared to the gift he received on the day he became a father.

And it'll make him glad.

Originally appeared in the Duluth News-Tribune *on Sunday, June 16, 1974.*

ONE FROM THE HEART FOR KATIE EIGHTY-EIGHT

When Sir Edward Elgar's now familiar *Pomp and Circumstance No. 1 in D Major* was given its debut performance in London in 1901, it achieved such instant popularity with the audience the conductor had to repeat the work three times before the crowd would leave the auditorium.

We know the main theme from the work as the tune we march down the aisle to when we graduate from high school. Virtually everyone in America, whether or not they appreciate orchestral music, can hum the "graduation song."

I was thinking about that first performance of *Pomp and Circumstance* the other night when I attended a high school commencement. The orchestra had to repeat the theme 17 or 18 times before all of the students were in their places.

After its very first performance, the work became enormously popular with the English people and someone penned words to the familiar march. The title and opening line became "Land of Hope and Glory" and it remains a patriotic anthem in Britain. So the march that accompanied English soldiers into battle accompanies American youth out to battle the world as they complete their formal schooling.

Elgar probably would have liked the way America uses his march, I sat thinking as the school orchestra repeated the theme over and over while an endless stream of capped-and-gowned graduates marched into the hall. My daughter was among them—the first of my children to graduate.

The words "land of hope and glory" kept running through my mind as the graduates marched. I always taught my children that they lived in a land of hope and glory, even if I didn't use those words, I sat musing as my foot tapped to the rhythm of the familiar march.

You can be anything you want to be, we tell our kids, if you work hard and use your talents. That's hope. What about the glory? It's out there, and it's worth striving for, we tell them. (Our office dictionary says glory is "great honor and admiration won by doing something important or valuable...") What parent hasn't dreamed that his or her child might achieve glory in some way? Then we all jog ourselves out of our dream—and hope the child will achieve the glory of a happy life, regardless of great honor and widespread admiration.

As the orchestra played on, and the graduates continued to file in, I looked around at other parents and loved ones in the audience straining to see their graduate, just as I was doing. I thought of my daughter's first day of school as a four-year-old. How her mother took her hand that first day and marched her down a street we regarded as too busy for our little girl to walk safely along. There was no pomp and circumstance that day 13 years ago, but there was plenty of hope and a good deal of glory as far as we were concerned. That was yesterday, I thought, as the rear guard entered the graduation hall, tassels bobbing on mortarboards.

For 15 years of writing this column, I have never used the actual names of my children or other members of my family. I'm going to break that tradition today. As our daughter moved through the grades in school, there came the day when we counted the years ahead to when she would graduate and realized she would be in the class of 1988.

Her nickname is Katie, and we began calling her Katie Eighty-eight. It has a ring to it—*Katie Eighty-eight.* One time she had an athletic jersey with her nickname at the top and the number 88 on the back. KT-88.

All this took place years ago, when 1988 seemed as remote as the year 2025 seems now. But suddenly there it was, the Class of '88 marching into the hall, Katie Eighty-eight among them as the orchestra played on. "Land of hope and glory…"

And when the program was over, the Class of '88 marched out (to a different melody), with all of us in the audience straining to see *our* graduate file into the real world that lay in the mists somewhere beyond the back of the arena. As she disappeared, I found myself thinking,

Here comes the world, Katie-Eighty-eight, it's full of glory.

And here comes Katie Eighty-eight, world, she's full of hope.

Originally appeared in the Duluth News-Tribune & Herald *on Sunday, June 12, 1988.*

REFLECTIONS WHILE WALKING BY A DEEP WOODS ON A DARK NIGHT

We're back to two of us against the world. Our youngest was graduated from high school last week in a flurry of excitement and activity that hardly gives a person time to reflect.

But inevitably you do reflect on such an occasion—maybe the next day or a couple of days later. With me it came as I walked the family dog after dark. We—the dog and I—stroll beside a large woods tucked right into our neighborhood like a bit of the wilderness. It's the kind of woods that inspired Robert Frost to write poetry, and strolling past its soaring evergreens with the dog often drains the daily cares from me and brings on reflection of my own.

It was at such a time after our son's graduation that the thought struck me: It's the two of us against the world again.

Let me explain.

You reach the point in life where something inside of you says that the best way to appreciate it is to share it with someone, so you get married. It's a pretty intrepid step, but you don't know it then. *We ain't got a barrel of money, but whether it's cloudy or sunny, we'll get along, singin' a song, side by side*—as the song goes.

It's the two of you against the world.

But as happens so often, nature intervenes, just as it's supposed to, and the two of you find out there will be a third. It's a time for jubilation—at least it was for us. It all happens so fast that you hardly remember when it was just the two of you against the world. You cradle that first baby in your arms and you know from now on it will be the three of us against the world.

In our case, it was the three of us against the world for two-and-a-half years—*just Molly and me, and baby makes three...in my blue heaven*—before we found out we would have a second child. Our daughter would have a sister and we were overjoyed (we had gotten used to baby girls). Our daughter got a brother. Taking a few seconds to adjust to the shock of having a boy join our trio, we enfolded him in our arms as well, and at that moment it became—you guessed it—the four of us against the world. For us that would be it.

It's difficult to convey to anyone who hasn't gone through it how rapidly the time passes. At the time that you establish yourself as a family unit against the world, you are incapable of understanding that it will ever come to an end. The enormous responsibility of parenthood is so pervasive, so overwhelming, that something inside tells you that it will go on forever. Nothing could ever interfere with this force. It is now, and ever shall be, the four of us against the world.

But that's not true. You start to realize it when those babies you are so zealous to protect are no longer babies. It comes when they reach about age 12. I mean it. In a parent's eyes they're babies until at least 12 and then maybe they're not babies, but they're not far beyond it.

An instant later for us—three years ago—our daughter was graduated from high school and off to college, still an adjunct to the family to be sure, but it left three of us against the world most of the time on the home front. And while the graduation of our son last week will not mean instant separation, the milestone signifies a time of breaking away and in reality we're back to the two of us against the world.

Twenty years ago, around the time all this started, I didn't know that there was any force on Earth that could divide a unit so strong as the four of us. But there is. What do you call it, nature? The same nature that created the stately dark woods the dog and I pass on our late night strolls? Or do you call it time, and is it the same thing?

Still, there's joy in knowing that those whom you have nurtured will be repeating that cycle. So you step aside—the two of you against the world once again—and let the next generation pass.

Originally appeared in the Duluth News-Tribune *on Sunday, June 9, 1991.*

THE BOYS WHO WENT TOO FAR ON THE BUS

*I*t's not easy being a pubescent punk. This is for the three boys who were kicked off the Duluth Transit Authority bus to the Woodland neighborhood one evening this week.

Boys, I just want you to know we adults understand how hard it is to be an adolescent. One day you're a cute little tyke getting your cheek pinched by grownups, and the next hairs start sprouting on that cheek and your voice goes crazy.

We understand all that, boys. We've been through it, too. It's no different for you than it was for us. That's why we understand when you get on the bus and stomp down the aisle with giant steps, hooting and hollering. You're just being fourteen.

We expect you'll go to the back of the bus, because that's where kids your age always sit—as far from the authority the driver represents as you can. No problem, boys. Somebody's got to sit back there.

And the rest of us on the bus, all of whom would have to be classified in the "grown up" category, understand when you make a lot of noise as we ride along.

The one of you whose voice has changed—that's a pretty good ape grunt you've perfected. It might strain our understanding a little bit that you never stop grunting, except to jab your buddy and utter certain vulgar words loud enough so the rest of us can hear. Still, we can handle that.

Nevertheless, all the grunting, jabbing, stomping and cussing is not comforting to the rest of us. Frankly, we're a little embarrassed for you. Do you have to be *that* fourteen? It makes the driver nervous, too. He's in charge of keeping order on the bus.

So we were a little relieved when the driver called to the back, "You boys want to get off right here?" Just a warning. Of course you knew that, didn't you boys?

Hey, that was cool—the way you ignored the driver's warning. What is he, a cop? A teacher? The principal? Heck no. You've learned already in life that you don't have to go around obeying bus drivers. Smart.

Besides, the ride wouldn't be the same without the incessant staccato of ape grunting, loud laughing, rib jabbing, mild cursing and general ruckus back there.

Your defiance worked, too, didn't it boys? The driver delivered the warning but he showed he's just another schlock adult authority figure by not backing it up. Maybe like your old man, huh boys?

Still, no real harm done until real harm was done, boys. I could see what happened coming half a block away as the bus slowly passed a boy on the sidewalk who wasn't as lucky as you boys on the bus. He was born with a physical handicap, one that caused spastic movement. Looked to be about your age, wouldn't you say bus boys?

A trio like you—cool guys—couldn't let that pass, could you? Ape grunting is OK when there's no spastic around to mock. Hey, look at that kid out there. He's different. He walks funny.

Here's where you went too far, boys. Yelling "retard, retard" through the open windows at the handicapped boy was not cool. It was cruel.

Incredibly cruel. If it reflects widespread attitudes of your generation it worries us. We don't understand that behavior. Not even from a pubescent punk with the world by the tail.

In case you're still wondering, that's what caused the driver to pull over to the side, unbuckle his seat belt, get out of his seat, stride back and order you off the bus.

You didn't want to leave, did you? Maybe it would make you late for supper. And, Mr. Ape Grunter Jr., your defiance of the driver was not impressive either.

You looked him in the eye and challenged: "What did I do?"

Not cool. Stupid question. Because if you don't know why you got kicked off the bus, you've got real problems, kid.

The older I get, the more I realize heroism is less caught up in grand gestures than in little things people with character will do because it's the right thing to do. So this last paragraph is to the driver of that bus, who stood by the back door and taught three boys a lesson we can only hope they learn, for their own sakes.

Way to go, driver.

Originally appeared in the Duluth News-Tribune *on Sunday, July 3, 1994.*

FOR MIDNITE—IT'S 5,000 DOG DAYS AND OUT

*I*t started with goldfish.

"Mommy, daddy, we want a pet," pleaded the kids. "Fine, we'll get some cute little goldfish," a parent responded.

So you buy a goldfish bowl, some fish food and a couple of goldfish and the first thing somebody does is feed them too many flakes and you wake up one morning and they don't. The children cry, you go out and get a couple more goldfish but they don't last very long either.

"What we need is a dog," suggests the older of the two kids. "Yeah, we need a dog," parrots the younger.

"No, we definitely do not need a dog," responds the grinch who thinks he wears the pants in the family. And, in a stroke of pure genius, he says, "What we need is a turtle."

The grinch explains that turtles live for a hundred years. "Longer than elephants." I had one when I was a kid that was supposed to get so old we optimistically named him Methuselah. That was a mistake, but he lasted longer than goldfish do.

Our kids bit on the turtle idea, so one Saturday we went in quest of a turtle. But we learned some disturbing news at the first pet store we went to. After asking the salesperson if we could see something in a turtle, he curtly informed us trading in turtles was against the law. "We haven't sold them in years. They spread salmonella."

This was news to me and bad news to my children. It prompted again the now familiar refrain, "What we need is a dog. Can't we get a dog? Please can't we get a dog?"

"No dogs," I held tough, explaining, "I have too much respect for dogs to keep them chained up all the time. Dogs are fine in the country, but not in the city. And that's final."

That quieted things down for maybe a month, but the subject of pets kept coming up. Some people move on to hamsters and gerbils, but we're just not rodent people. Finally, I relented and we checked the classified ads for a dog. We found one ("part poodle, part spitz, part terrier"), wrote the sellers a check for $20 and packed a little black ball of fur into the car with the promise it wouldn't grow any bigger than the mother. That was 13 years ago last January.

Last week we put him "to sleep," an ailing, tired and worn-out pooch that could no longer take nourishment or even stand on his own. I don't have to tell dog owners and dog lovers how that makes you feel. Others will never understand.

So today I write with a heavy heart for a dog we named Midnite (spelling it that way intentionally) when he was a jet black puppy, but early in life his coat got more gray, prompting someone to remark, "He looks more like 11:30."

It really has been 11:30 for Midnite for the last six months or so. He developed heart problems last year and we started him on medicine for that, but he slowly began to lose quality of life. His horizons became increasingly limited (no more roving the house upstairs and down, leaping up on furniture, or going on long walks).

How many days in 13 years have I looked at Midnite and thought how lucky dogs are. We humans have to go out, deal with the world, earn a living, worry about this and that, and all they have to do is lie around the house all day. That was true most of the 5,000 or so days Midnite lived, but not last Sunday. That day, with the merciful help of a veterinarian, Midnite had to do what every living creature must eventually do.

As we drove away from the vet's office after seeing him through to the end, an odd thought struck me—how every spring we had to buy heartworm pills for him. Do you know about heartworm? Unless you ward it off with medicine, dogs pick up a parasite that worms its way into the heart muscle, seriously weakening it. Midnite didn't have heartworm, but I was wondering if there's a pill for human heartworm.

What's human heartworm? You get a dog and he worms his way into your heart, and when he dies you realize he's leaving a void that I suppose time will eventually fill. But it'll be a while.

Originally appeared in the Duluth News-Tribune *on Wednesday, June 8, 1994.*

FATHER OF THE GROOM

*T*hey've made movies about fathers of the bride, but what about the father of the groom at weddings? He's always portrayed, if he's portrayed at all, as an oafish interloper who gets in the way of nuptial progress with embarrassing suggestions.

The highlight of my recent absence from my job (normally called a "vacation") was a family wedding in which my role was father of the groom.

The father of the groom looks like the other male members of the wedding party (tux, boutonniere, patent leather shoes, patented grin, etc.), but he has no real duties. The father of the bride gets to march his daughter down the aisle and present her to the groom, a dramatic moment that only falls just short of the vows themselves.

The father of the groom watches—granted from a good seat behind home plate.

To out-of-town and other guests who don't know him, the father of the groom is this stranger in formal dress they must pay attention to, but they're not quite sure why. ("Who's that dude?")

Because I have been through this so recently, it seems like a good idea to offer future fathers of the groom some insights, and it's also a good time to revisit a recurring theme of this column: the precipitous rise of hugging in America.

It's out of control, and—guess what?—that is what the father of the groom does. He hugs. Since he's all gussied up in a tux, he is fair prey for the huggers of the world, and they are everyone else.

As I've pointed out here in the past, I am an awkward hugger. I can't help it; it's the way I'm made. My main hugging problem is that while at the perigee of the embrace, I uncontrollably pat the poor hugees on the back with my left hand, causing their voices to break and wobble if they are saying anything, such as, "So nice to meet you," or, "Back off, masher, or I'm calling 911 on my cell."

I feel sorry for petite women who find themselves hugged by me and have the wind knocked out of them.

Still, as father of the groom you might as well resign yourself to a lot of hugging. To be cordial, I even initiated hugs, enfolding mainly women—but a few men as well—into my husky arms, my out-of-control left hand beating them on the back to the point of their requiring oxygen.

I hugged everybody in sight. No one was safe. I hugged on introductions. I hugged on farewells. I hugged on general principles. I hugged strangers (hug first, ask questions later). I hugged people I knew well but never hugged before. I became a hugging fool.

Even with that experience now behind me, I still doubt that I'll ever be a relaxed and natural hugger. Too many pitfalls, like when I hugged the janitor sweeping up the reception hall. What a moment: father of the groom hugging wielder of the broom.

Quick, grab a camera.....

Originally appeared in the Duluth News Tribune *on Sunday, September 2, 2001.*

CONFESSIONS OF A NEW GRANDFATHER

I have been observing my grandchildren as they develop from babyhood to toddler. We have four, some in each of those age categories or somewhere in between.

It's hard to tell when they stop being babies and start being toddlers. One day they're helpless infants, the next they're toddlers and before you know it they graduate from high school—all but the latter in diapers.

We are dealing with a quartet of little lives, three, including a set of twins, hovering around the age of one and now able to stand on their own two feet, and the eldest, the only girl in the bunch, pushing three and soon to eschew Kimberly-Clark for Fruit of the Loom, everyone hopes.

All grandparents say the same things about having grandchildren: How they can't imagine how they did it as parents ("did it" meaning how much work and worry parenting is), and what a relief it is to be able to check in and out of their grandchildren's lives without having total responsibility.

I guess that's true. Being a grandparent also affords the opportunity to observe the children's development in a slightly more detached manner. When you're the parent, you're constantly running from pillar to post just getting them fed, changed, rested and safe. You don't get a chance to even think about the baby-steps in their development until they reach one of their big milestones (tooth, walk, talk, Ph.D.) and you wonder what went before it.

And you realize, when you are able to view all this from two generations up, that there's plenty going on that you were too busy with day-to-day operations to notice when you were rearing your own kids.

It seems to me that children of this early age must approach each new day as truly new: "So this is what life is all about," they're thinking today. Not what it was all about yesterday.

Somebody wrote, "The cowboy, like the duck, wakes up to a brand new world every morning." That's what small children are like. Oh, they might learn some new little skill one day and retain it the next, but there's so much new to take in every day, the past is nothing, the present is everything and the future doesn't exist. And it won't for several years.

When we entertain our grandchildren at home, we must cover every electrical outlet, bar bookcases from reach, protect knobs on the stereo, remove the lowest photos from the refrigerator door, seal low kitchen cabinets and then wait to find out what else will be needed to protect them…and us. The piano is being subjected to its third generation of toddler pounding, including my own, and it's music to my ears.

I recommend grandchildren. We were a little late in acquiring them, but far better late than never. Some of my friends have grandchildren finishing high school while we eagerly await a few recognizable words and full sentences, or the milestones of a somersault, a swim or balancing on a bike.

It's fun to observe, but I hope it doesn't go too fast. There's no hurry to move beyond cowboy or duck, when you wake up to a brand new world every morning. Take it from me—I'm still that way.

Originally appeared in the Duluth News Tribune *on Sunday, July 29, 2007.*

PART IV:

THE ETHNIC EDITOR

THE ETHNIC EDITOR

No collection of my columns would be complete without including a sampling of my voluminous writings on matters ethnic. Voluminous is right, but here are six that cover several years of ethnic commentary, almost none of it serious.

At some point I declared myself the newspaper's award-winning "Ethnic Editor" and "The Dean of Twin Ports Ethnic Editors," which is hard to say with your tongue lodged firmly in your cheek. I don't know of a newspaper in the United States that actually employs an ethnic editor, but if any does, he or she should be put back on obituaries.

Most of these columns reflect, in a light-hearted way, the competitiveness I sensed between people in this area of Swedish and Norwegian extraction when I was growing up among Swedes but near Norwegians. That competitiveness hardly exists today. I found that poking fun at it was well received by Norwegian-Americans, who were always the target. I appreciated their understanding that I meant no harm. Besides, the old early 20th Century chauvinism has pretty much died out today, as recent generations have moved beyond divisions of religion and ethnic origin among immigrants—to the point where we can all laugh at those old attitudes.

The first two columns in this chapter involve a "threat" I once made to pick up everything and actually move to Norway. My mode of transportation? Walking. That started as a satire of an announcement at the time by a well-known Minnesota writer that he was moving to Denmark, but many readers actually believed I was moving to Norway. I'm afraid I only got as far as the Twin Cities, but it was fun along the way.

Finally, there's lutefisk, a "delicacy" shared by both Swedes and Norwegians, and a tempting target for ethnic editors. This one couldn't resist.

THE FIRST FINAL FAREWELL
BEFORE LEAVING FOR NORWAY

Well, it's been nice, and I really appreciate the support you folks have given me over the years, but I've decided to leave all this behind and move to Norway.

Now hold it. Don't feel badly. I'll miss you readers more than you'll miss me, but there comes a time in a person's life—especially the life of a somewhat public person—when he needs to pull back and lead his own life. Especially a shy public person, although I hate to use the word shy, it having been appropriated, so maybe bashful will suffice.

It's no secret it's been difficult around here lately after one, then a second, telephone book published my address and also my telephone number. And then when the upstart phone book threw in the zip code, well, nobody asked me if it was OK.

Sometimes a person just wants to be left alone in his "home" town. I hate to sound bitter but, when the city directory went ahead and published detailed information concerning my employment and the like, not to mention the vital statistics of my address—that pushed me over the edge.

So it's goodbye Blanche (regular readers will remember that infamous name), and farewell Answer Man—she's really a woman—who answers the questions people are asking about the important issues of the day (and night).

I'll miss mean-old Blanche and laconic Answer Man, though—more than you will. The thing to remember is that I'll miss you more than you'll miss me. I know you hate to see me go. But there comes a time for a bashful person to get on with it.

Why Norway? Norway is out of the mainstream, a place where a person can really blend in and be bland, which bashful people like myself really crave, although it sometimes doesn't seem like it when we do stuff to call attention to ourselves. This is overcompensation for the bashfulness we all feel on the inside. That's why Norway seems like just the right place, even though I haven't got a drop of Norwegian blood in my arteries.

The Norwegian Norwegians aren't at all like the American Norwegians anyway. The Norwegian Norwegians are sure of themselves and their place in the world order—and are satisfied with it. They aren't tense about getting lapped by the Laps. It's American Norwegians who are the Scandinavian hotshots, not the Norwegian Norwegians.

I don't want to tear down the descendants of the land I am going to adopt, though. I just hope to make it clear why I am totally withdrawing from a life I have known for so long. And I wanted to say farewell to those loyal readers who have been so supportive over the years.

Actually, there isn't enough room in one column to say farewell properly, so I'll probably say farewell some more on Sunday (this column runs Wednesdays and Sundays). Maybe another farewell column next Wednesday will be needed also to express my appreciation to you readers, whom I'll miss a lot more than you'll miss me.

In fact, I'm starting to miss you so much just thinking about it that I may have to have a third farewell column a week from Sunday, to be followed by a fourth farewell a week from Wednesday, which will bring us through half of June, almost to my annual patriotic Independence Day column, so I might as well not say final farewell until then, but if I do—we bashful are hard to predict—I'll agree to come back and do my Independence Day piece everyone looks forward to so much.

After that, though, it's off to Norway with me forever, or I might come back in August, who can say? If I do, though, I'll be sure and check in with the readers, even if it is to say one final farewell, which should get us into autumn, when everything starts up again around here.

It could be I will be persuaded to come out of seclusion for a final farewell in the fall, maybe not. We'll just have to take it one day at a time. Fact is, I might not go to Norway at all. I don't know. So farewell. Maybe. We'll see.

Originally appeared in the Duluth News-Tribune *on Wednesday, May 24, 1989.*

Intrepid Traveler to Norway Detained in Minneapolis

When I got disgusted with life in Duluth and announced in May I was going to move to Norway, I had no idea I'd still be traveling in December. Even walking, you'd think I'd be doing better than I am.

Health nuts and crazed fund-raising campaigners sometimes walk great distances—like across the entire country—in the time I have spent so far in walking to Norway and here I am only in the Twin Cities area.

Perhaps you remember back when I announced I was leaving the United States because I was fed up with American culture, or American no-culture. I longed for a simpler, quieter life away from the hubbub of late 20th Century Fox. (They don't make movies the way they used to, either.)

I was sick and tired of being in the public eye and felt betrayed when the telephone directory printed my name and address. And Norway to me represents the very antithesis of fast-lane living in America. In Norway I figured I could wear colorful sweaters all the time, spend my days on skis and my nights folk dancing around roaring hearths.

But it hasn't been easy getting there, and I have all-but given up hope of making it to Norway by Christmas, the most festive season of all, when they serve all those foods nobody can spell because several letters have dots over them.

How I got to the Twin Cities is interesting, but first I have to mention that Norwegian Norwegians aren't uppity like American Norwegians, so that's no problem if you move there. Norwegian Norwegians don't think they're better than everyone else. They know they're not. Show me a European people who know their place and I'll show you a people whose American relatives are uppity. They send their kids to St. Olaf and think they're hot stuff.

The worst thing that ever happened was the merging of the Norwegian and Swedish Lutheran churches in America recently. Now the Norwegians will take over and the Swedes will all go to hell, although that's church politics, a subject area I have always tried to stay away from because I value my bones.

Yes, how I made it to the Twin Cities is interesting, but first I'd like to mention that my friends who are of Norwegian extraction shouldn't take umbrage at anything I say about Norwegians here, especially if they are surly drinkers. Now, on to the Twin Cities, where I am writing this.

But first a little background: This is the third route I have attempted in walking to Norway. First I tried Highway 2 over to Ashland, Wis., but was turned back by bad weather. Then I tried Highway 53 to Spooner but was turned back by giant 600-pound marauding wolf-dogs who were feeding on shepherds in the fields while they watched their flocks by night. So I figured I'd better stick to Minnesota, even if it is out of the way, and set out on old Highway 61 through Atkinson, Mahtowa, Barnum, Moose Lake, Sturgeon Lake (home of St. Isidore's), Willow River and points south.

I made it to the Twin Cities shortly after Thanksgiving right when they were decorating the shopping malls for Christmas (and Hanukkah, or Chanukkah, to be fair to both spellings). It's such a big place it's hard to walk through, and it wasn't long before undercover Minneapolis cops noticed I looked suspicious so they tried to buy drugs from me.

I offered to sell them a couple of aspirins and they took me for some kind of nut and had me detained at the station, allowing me only one telephone call. I called the Dayton's gift advisory service and they suggested I purchase a Santa Bear 1989, but I decided not to because it will be outdated a week after Christmas.

Habeas corpus got me out of the clink, and now I am at the Sons of Norway headquarters on Lake Street or Minnetonka Boulevard, depending on your income. They don't know what to do with me either, but they have to take care of me because they know I'm committed to Norway, which is better than being committed to Moose Lake, let me tell you.

Originally appeared in the Duluth News-Tribune *circa December, 1989.*

Peace Could be Threatened
on the Scandinavian Peninsula

*M*any people thought I was just poking a little fun when I wrote about the competition between American Swedes and Norwegians for "Best Scandinavian Nationality."

A few years ago when I threatened to move to Norway, and when I made some public comments about the rivalry between people in this area who consider themselves one of the two nationalities, non-Scandinavians thought I was making it all up. Second-generation Serbs and Croatians who live in northern Minnesota couldn't understand why people so alike as Norwegians and Swedes couldn't get along better.

But I wasn't kidding. Of course, the rivalry was keener in earlier generations. They wouldn't even worship together in the earlier days—each choosing a slightly different brand of Lutheranism with which to assure their eternal salvation. From what I understand, though, a lot of both sides made it to heaven when they died—and some of both didn't.

Most of the Norwegians and Swedes around here today are the sons and daughters and even grandchildren and great-grandchildren of the original Swedes and Norwegians who settled here after immigrating from their native lands. That's how I got to be a half-Swede. One set of grandparents came over on the *Wallflower* (no dancing in the Swedish Lutheran Church).

So the resentment between the two has diminished somewhat as intermarriage and passing decades separate today's generation from the traditions of the old country, whichever old country you're affiliated with.

But the Norwegians still think they're hot stuff. Everybody knows that.

As the late, great John L. Lewis, perhaps the greatest eyebrow grower in the history of the American labor movement but a non-Scandinavian, once said: "He who tooteth not his own horn, the same shall not be tooted."

The Norwegians understand that better than the Swedes—and good for them. The Norwegians have prospered in the new land, while the king of Sweden back in Stockholm can't even afford cable TV, it was reported in the paper this week.

(Special note to Swedish King Carl XVI Gustaf: The way cable rates are rising in Duluth, I'm starting to wonder if I can afford it, too. P.S. I hate to bring this up but most monarchs put their number *after* their full name, like Henry VIII, Louis XIV and Elizabeth II, and so do popes, like John XXIII. If you continue to put your number in the middle, Norwegians will laugh at you. Thanks, king.)

It would be easy to mention lutefisk here, but let's get to the point.

Just when everybody thought I was nuts when I wrote about the rivalry, the last week produced two letters to the editor in this newspaper which—sad to say—revealed that the rivalry and resentment has not gone away a century after the great first influx of Scandinavians to the Upper Midwest.

The first letter took the *News Tribune* to task for printing a list of new year's greetings in several languages, including the Norwegian greeting but not the Swedish. The writer said, why use Norway as the example when Sweden is the dominant nation of the Scandinavian peninsula? Norway used to be a minor province of Sweden, the writer claimed.

It didn't take long for a Norwegian sympathizer to answer. He questioned the claim of dominance and said that, after World War II, Norwegians and Danes (he brought the Danes into this, I didn't; but I think Danes are great) would have nothing to do with the Swedes and that bad feelings persist even today.

Well, what do you think of that? Bad feelings between Swedes and Norwegians exist today? So was I crazy?

Let's hope it doesn't get so bad that one invades the other and America will have to go over there and draw a line in the snow. Swedes and Norwegians everywhere should always remember that they're all the same in the eyes of Thor.

Originally appeared in the Duluth News-Tribune *on Sunday, January 13, 1991.*

THERE'S NO PLACE LIKE NORWAY
FOR THE HOLIDAYS

*O*h, how I long to be in Norway, when Christmastime is nigh, with snow festooning towering pines, wind wafting through the olive trees as gaily dressed women dance around cozy, candle-lit kitchens baking traditional dishes in wood-fired ovens, and the livin' is easy; the catfish are jumpin' and soon rotting in lye.

> *I love Oslo in the springtime, I love Oslo in the fall;*
> *I love Oslo in the summer, when it sneezes,*
> *I love Oslo in the winter, when it freezes.*
> *The last time I saw Trondheim, its heart was young and gay...*
> *It's a long way to Bergen, Norway, it's a long way to go...*

Oh, excuse me. I get carried away about Norway at this time of year. Forgive an old fool for longing for the land of his dreams at holiday time. Not being there for Christmas is the hardest, when thoughts of the old country come rushing forth at the slightest prompting—a Norwegian carol, perhaps, or the chance of meeting a know-it-all.

Not that I've actually ever been to Norway at Christmastime. Not that I've ever been there at all. I haven't. But I know all about it and decided years ago that it's the country I'd settle in if only I had half a chance, in spite of being a half-baked Swede myself.

As regular readers can readily attest, I have made several attempts to move to Norway, lock, stock and barrel, but something always stops me. I'm beginning to think it is a Norwegian curse of some kind—like the Curse of the Vampire in Transylvania. I know that Count Dracula, who sometimes took the form of a bat, never had anything to do with Norway, thank heaven, but how do you explain the Norwegian rat? If there are two things we Norwegian chauvinists want to forget they are Vidkun Quisling and the Norwegian rat. You won't hear Norwegians brag about them, although they'll brag about just about everything else—American-Norwegians, I mean.

Something happened to them on the boat over, or in the birth canal, that turned humble, fun-loving, folk dancing country folk in the old country into the Scandinavian hotshots in the United States. They go around claiming they discovered America and boasting about how good they are at cross-country skiing.

But not Norwegian Norwegians. They know they have the best country on Earth—no need to tell anybody about it. They quietly go about their business, respecting their royal family, King Oscar and Queen Sonja. Not like in England where scandals in the royal family rock the nation, causing poor Queen Elizabeth to have such a bad year she agreed to pay income taxes.

There is not a breath of scandal in the palace of Norway's King Oscar and Queen Sonja, except that time when King Oscar wore brown shoes with blue knickerbockers. As far as taxes are concerned, King Oscar and Queen Sonja are happy to pay taxes to help their country. As the Norrona Gnome, official publication of the Superior Sons of Norway chapter, noted in Norwegian, *Det er flere sorn spor etter rikdom enn etter visdom.*

Translation: "It is wise to get your digestive system checked before they send you flowers."

Oh, but I go on bragging, just like the real American Norwegians. This is not the season for bragging, 'tis the season of joy.

On behalf of Norwegians everywhere, let me wish everyone, even those darn Swedes, a *God Jul.* That's Norwegian for Merry Christmas, and it's also the way the Swedes put it.

The actual translation of *God Jul* is Good Yule. Although it's been said many times, many ways, *God Jul, God Jul* to you.

Norwegians are very poetic, too.

Originally appeared in the Duluth News-Tribune *on Wednesday, December 16, 1992.*

My Life in Lutefisk

*J*ust because I'm the *Duluth News Tribune*'s ethnic editor, I'm suddenly responsible for lutefisk? They turn to me when lutefisk questions come up, and I don't even like the stuff.

For the sake of honest reporting, today I present my lutefisk manifesto, my magnum lutefisk opus, which I have titled, "My Life in Lutefisk."

It's true I have been exposed to lutefisk throughout my life, but I was vaccinated at an early age.

Last week when editors here asked me to compare other ethnic foods to lutefisk—such as lutefisk is to Norwegians what (some other food) is to (some other country)—I came up with some pretty bad stuff, but I forgot to include that "lutefisk is to Norwegians what death is to normal human beings."

Actually, lutefisk is not the sole property of Norwegians at all. Norwegians seem to claim it, but Swedes prepared lutefisk, too. Some experts, many of them now deceased, can tell you the difference between Norwegian and Swedish lutefisk.

But back to my life in lutefisk. My mother, who was a first-generation Swedish-American (both of her parents were born in Sweden), made lutefisk from a recipe no doubt brought from the old country. It was frequently served in our home when I was a child, and my father, who had no Scandinavian blood whatsoever, learned to like it—even relish it. But then he liked things like oyster stew, too.

Let the record show that when served lutefisk as a child I did not throw up. I tried to eat it, heaping plenty of mustard on it to cover up the taste. But a woman can only take so much griping before she gets discouraged, so my mother, when preparing lutefisk, would throw on a few Swedish meatballs for us kids. I wasn't too nuts about Swedish meatballs either (they had onion mixed in), but at least they weren't life threatening.

My mother knew enough not to serve lutefisk on Christmas, as had been the custom in the home she grew up in. Mercifully, the family had converted to turkey before I arrived.

Now we jump ahead a few decades in my life in lutefisk. I am married with children of my own and haven't tasted lutefisk in many years. My wife and children have never tasted it.

My mother, now widowed and elderly, invites us for Sunday dinner and I suggest she make lutefisk so my family could try it. I believe in providing children with all kinds of experiences. How are children supposed to know what foods taste bad if they've never tried the worst?

"I'll put on a few meatballs too, just in case the kids don't like lutefisk," said mom.

For my part, I was intrigued to try her lutefisk again. I thought maybe my palate would take to it better now that I was older. So mom served a steaming plate of white lutefisk and we all dug in.

You like to be polite at a time like that. After all, somebody's gone to a lot of bother—at your request. So you try.

After sampling the delicacy, my wife and kids had that funny look people get on their faces when they aren't sure if they're smelling the WLSSD or something very, very personal.

"Well," mom asked, "what does everybody think?"

She received an indirect answer: "Pass the meatballs."

Originally appeared in the Duluth News-Tribune *on Sunday, December 10, 1995.*

BAD NEWS FROM ABROAD

*O*h boy, we no sooner get the Taliban on the run in Afghanistan and out comes the bad news that Norway has been named the No. 1 place in the world to live.

Well, I guess you've got to take the bad along with the good. Now there'll be no living with American Norwegians, or, as they would put it themselves, Norwegian Americans. Must put Norway first.

News last Sunday that the United Nations Human Development Report has declared Norway the best place to live on the planet had them dancing in the aisles of Norwegian Lutheran churches in the Midwest, and was cause for wild celebration at stately Norway Hall in downtown Duluth. You'd have thought it was wedding day at Trollhaugen.

At a Sunday afternoon session of the *Nordmannsforbundit* (literal translation: blonde guys), the ecstatic board of elders toasted with a second cup of strong coffee before they made plans to lord it over every non-

Norwegian they know, especially those of Swedish extraction, like me. I'm a half Swede, half Marsupial, which is as good an excuse as I know of to go around half in the bag.

Those gull-darn Norwegians think they're the Scandinavian Hot-shots and they won't let you forget it. Now they get this vote of confidence (as if they need any more confidence). It's discouraging.

A couple of weeks ago I got a call from an 86-year-old reader of Swedish stock who asked me when I was going to again address the Norwegian "problem." That used to be a recurring theme in this column, but I moved away from it when I almost got punched in the snot locker by a bald Norwegian at the Miller Hall Mill.

Since then, I've tried to visit other subjects in my ongoing efforts to further world peace, foster the brotherhood of man, look after the welfare of poor widows and children, feed the 5,000 homeless on Thanksgiving, turn fish into wine, and wash the feet of prisoners in the county jail. But you can only have so much faith, hope and sweet charity before you get pushed to the breaking point and can remain silent no longer.

This has done it, and in the season of sacred lutefisk, which the Norwegians claim they invented when they know all well and good the Swedes invented it. Give them credit for ishy lefse—they can have it—but when it comes to lutefisk, they have to take a back seat to Sweden, although no Norwegian has ever sat in the back seat for very long.

Not that I personally can eat lutefisk without throwing up, unless I smear lots of Salsa Dem Darhemma Sauce on it. But credit should be given where credit is due, by golly, and it is the Swedes who gave lutefisk to the world, just as they gave the world dynamite, making modern warfare and stump removal possible.

Many of my relations have been so proud of me for rising to the lofty position of ethnic editor at this newspaper, and winning many outstanding awards for my distinguished work in ethnicity, but do I mention it? Never. Give that job to a Norwegian and find out what boasting is all about. I take the mantle of Dean of Twin Ports Ethnic Editors with a pillar of saltpeter.

And another thing: Pickled herring. Need I say more?

In conclusion, I hope the United Nations realizes it has set Swedish-Norwegian relations back 1,000 years, to the days of Osama Adolphus, with this reckless designation.

Originally appeared in the Duluth News Tribune *on Sunday, May 25, 2001.*

PART V:

THE RICH & FAMOUS COLLIDE WITH DULUTH

THE RICH & FAMOUS
COLLIDE WITH DULUTH

One of the attractions of newspaper work is that at times it can provide opportunities to have contact with the high and the mighty, the rich and the famous, the egocentric and the vainglorious, the talented and the not-so.

It was difficult to select columns for this chapter because so many interesting luminaries had to be left out, such as Jack Benny. Is he still remembered? I interviewed him years ago in Duluth. Same with Maurice Chevalier, once a famous Frenchman, now hardly remembered.

This chapter does include some whose names likely are instantly recognizable to most people. I couldn't resist sharing a take-off on Calvin Griffith (not that well known today, granted) in the spirit of "Casey at the Bat." As then owner of the Minnesota Twins, one week in 1978 he hit the front pages of the state's newspapers after a disastrous speech before a southern Minnesota service club in which he shocked his audience with comments on marriage, race and some of his then-famous players. In short, the mighty Calvin struck out.

The column on Hubert Humphrey won first place in its category in the 1979 Page One Awards competition sponsored by the Minnesota Society of Professional Journalists and the Newspaper Guild of the Twin Cities. It speaks from the grave about the fortunes of Humphrey's party at that time.

Also from the world of politics, I've included a column written on the day Minnesota Senator Paul Wellstone was killed in an airplane crash. It was written in the afternoon of that fateful day, during a time when I and other members of the *News Tribune* editorial board were scheduled to meet with him. Readers will recognize all the rest, especially Elvis. Although I never interviewed him, I got within speaking range. He just didn't talk.

CALVIN GRIFFITH:
CALVIN AT THE PLATE

The outlook wasn't brilliant for the Lions Club that day;
The chaplain muffed the praying and the Lions would have to pay.
And so when Calvin took the stand, and after they had dined,
The Lions sat back to listen up, looking leonine.

The subject would be baseball, appropriately enough,
But who could know the speaker would be dishing out such guff;
A simple little meeting, in a simple little town,
Would make the club look foolish and the speaker look a clown.

But Calvin didn't know that day the ripples he would cause;
He tried his best to stand the test and gather up applause.
But his audience included, much to his distress,
A writer taking lots of notes, and he was from the press.

So when Calvin started talking, and missing not a point,
The air was filled with silence, and smoke filled up the joint.
The speaker tried for laughter, and getting himself none,
He thought he'd toss some spice around, to add it to the fun.

He started out with marriage, an honorable state,
But Calvin said it had no place on or near home plate;
He said his catcher Wynegar would be better off still free:
He didn't care that Wynegar's wife would deign to disagree.

Free love, he said, comes pretty cheap for players of the game;
A lad should take advantage, and build upon his name,
And then when extra innings in the game of life are played,
There's plenty of time for marriage, when life's a bit more staid.

There was ease in Calvin's manner as he shifted on his hips;
There was pride in Calvin's bearing, and a smile on Calvin's lips;
There was scotch in Calvin's belly, and a redness on his face,
When Calvin turned the subject to a place known as first base.

His voice boomed like thunder when he talked of Rod Carew;
And everyone was shocked when he called him a damn fool.
Rod sold himself too cheap, he said, so we gave him a bonus;
He really should appreciate such treatment from the owners.

Then Calvin changed his visage, his voice a quiet roar;
"In the old days players cared," he cried, "but they don't any more."
And throwing out an epithet, the kind we know so well,
He told the stadium commission that it could go to hell.

And hitting Billy Martin—he couldn't let that pass—
He said the feisty manager could charm a monkey's _ _ _.
And he said Bill never punched a man who looked to be his size;
He'll have to live with that one, until the day he dies.

And then as if to top the rest, ol' Cal went on to say,
The team could leave tomorrow, but it's still here today
Because we moved from Washington, balls, bats, gloves and sacks,
When we heard that Minnesota had but fifteen thousand blacks.

Oh! Somewhere in this favored land the sun is shining bright,
The band is playing somewhere, and somewhere hearts are light;
And somewhere men are laughing, and somewhere children shout,
But there was no joy in Twinsville, when Calvin G. spoke out.

Originally appeared in the Duluth News-Tribune *on Sunday, October 8, 1978.*

HUBERT HUMPHREY:
HEAVEN KNOWS, ANYTHING GOES

I went to a séance the other night with a group of people trying to contact spirits from the beyond.

On this night, they were trying to contact Herbert Hoover by repeating his initials over and over again in the dark. These were politically conservative spiritualists, and they wanted Hoover's advice on what to do about the economy.

It came as quite a shock to most of us when, instead of Herbert Hoover, who shows up but Hubert Humphrey. Apparently heaven got its wires crossed when it heard the call for H.H., and sent H.H.H. instead.

All the better, I thought, although I'm not sure my companions felt comfortable with anybody as liberal as Humphrey. But since it was a day after the recent midterm election, I saw it as a rare opportunity to interview the late vice president and Minnesota U.S. senator for the paper.

And as was the case when he walked among us, Hubert was ready and willing to sit down and talk to a reporter.

"Tell us, Senator Humphrey, what's it like up there? Are you happy?" I asked.

"You don't have to call me Senator Humphrey now any more than you did before," he responded. "I'm Hubert; always will be. And I mean always. But to answer your question, it's great up here. It's just like I was trying to make it down there when I was with you folks."

"Do they still call you the Happy Warrior?"

"Well, no, not exactly. There's no such thing as war up here so there're no warriors. But I am happy. That I am. Yes, very, very happy. As happy as could be. Yes, that's right."

I could see that he still repeated everything he said three times before leaving a subject.

"I hate to bring this up, Senator, but...."

"Call me Hubert."

"Ah yes, Hubert. I hate to bring this up, but I suppose you know what happened in Minnesota in last week's election."

"I know very well what happened. They don't keep any secrets from us up here. That's the nice thing about this place; you don't have to depend on newspapers for information."

"Then I guess you know what happened to the DFL Party in the election. It was virtually swept from office."

"You don't have to tell me something I already know, son. I know what happened. But I don't feel sorry for any of 'em, not Wendy, not Rudy, not any of them."

"But don't you feel a little rueful that the party you forged and nurtured for 30 years has gone down in ignominious defeat at the hands of the Republicans?"

"Well, son, let me put it this way. It's never been my style to sit around and cry over things you can't do anything about. No sense in that. Look what happened to me in the presidential election in 1968. A few votes the other way and I would have been president."

He paused to catch his breath, then continued. "All through this latest campaign these fellows—and Fritz too—kept on invoking my name, trying to get votes with my name even though I'm not there any more. Big crowds would gather and they'd have moments of silence for me. Me! I never saw a moment of silence in my whole lifetime.

"No, instead of going out and getting votes for themselves, they called this 'Humphrey country' and told people about the 'Humphrey tradition.' Bunk. I never won an election in my life on the coattails of someone who's gone. Not Hubert Humphrey.

"If those fellows are going to win any elections in the future, they're going to have to do it on their own. They're going to have to make their own traditions and lay claim to their own country for their own reasons. I had my chance and I think I did pretty well, if you don't mind my saying so."

Finally, he started to fade and I knew we were going to lose contact.

"I see I have to leave again now," Hubert said, "but I'll be back in the fall of 1980, you can bet on that. I wouldn't miss an election for the life of me. Well, not the life of me, I guess. Not any more. And that's what the party is going to have to understand. They're going to have to learn to get along without me."

With that, he faded into the dimness. "Good luck," I called after him.

"Thanks, I'll need it. I'm running for gatekeeper."

Originally appeared in the Duluth News-Tribune *on Sunday, November 12, 1978.*

BUDDY HOLLY:
THREE DAYS BEFORE THE ROCK STARS DIED

*E*very time it comes up—and it keeps coming up more often as time passes—I find myself somewhat of an oddity among younger people when I tell them I was there the night Buddy Holly, Ritchie Valens and the Big Bopper played Duluth three nights before they died in a plane crash.

When a movie based on Holly's life was released a few years ago, there was a lot of talk about the Duluth connection. Now the movie *La Bamba*, which portrays Valens' life and career, is showing here.

Many people from around here know the entertainers played Duluth shortly before they met their deaths in Iowa, but I am not aware that anyone has written a first-person account of it. So that is what I am up to today. These are just my recollections—and impressions—of the occasion. Memory is not always accurate, but this is how I saw it.

It was Saturday night, January 31, 1959, that the "Winter Dance Party" played the old Duluth Armory on London Road. My friend Lew Latto, now owner of several local and area radio stations, promoted the concert. He met the performers. I was just in the audience.

The program was one of a succession of "Armory dances" held in those days and they drew big crowds of teenagers. The audience did not sit down. The Armory floor was left clear for dancing. Holly and Valens, along with the Big Bopper, were all hit artists at the time. Duluth often gets entertainers on the way up, on the way down or on the way to nowhere. These guys were somewhere right then. They were on the charts, and they were here in person.

Everyone was aware it was a special Armory dance because of that. Holly was the headliner, but Valens had made such a hit with his tune "La Bamba" he wasn't very far behind. If you were young and in Duluth that night, there was absolutely nowhere else to be. I was a 19-year-old UMD student, and half the campus was at the dance.

Reading old newspaper clips, I see that Dion and the Belmonts were on the program, too, but I don't remember them. And I only vaguely recall the Big Bopper as a novelty act. He was supposed to be funny and yelled a lot ("Chantilly Lace!").

The social dynamics at those dances, it need hardly be pointed out, involved meeting members of the opposite sex as much as artistic appreciation—probably more. The dances were largely attended by boys and girls (young men and women) who would go "stag." For many, like myself, the performance was secondary to the other. Maybe lightning would strike and you'd meet the love of your life, the thinking went. Maybe not, life often shot back. It was the '50s.

Anyway, I remember standing maybe 75 feet from the stage during the performances. The girls went absolutely gaga over Holly—screaming, jumping, clapping. When he sang "Peggy Sue," the place went wild. I couldn't figure out what the girls saw in him. Dressed in a sport-coat and tie, he wore horn-rim glasses and had a mop of dark hair, but he was as plain as the Texas countryside from which he had sprung.

I couldn't understand all the fuss.

Valens was a classic Latin type—black hair, even features—but I thought he was kind of chubby for a singing idol. He wore black, but it didn't hide his baby fat (he was only 17). He had a great song in "La Bamba" and, once again, the crowd went wild. But as with Holly, I couldn't understand why the girls were so crazy for him.

Holly and Valens must have had something, though. I went to a lot of those Armory dances, and that is the only one I can remember so clearly. Perhaps it is because three days later the news broke that they had been killed. It was the Tuesday after the Saturday Duluth performance.

Everyone around UMD's Kirby Student Center was talking about it in hushed tones. The reaction of young people to death is often emotionally askew, but I don't remember anybody crying or hugging.

One boy I was talking to about it that morning captured the moment. I think I can quote him precisely: "Why did it have to be Buddy Holly? Why couldn't it have been me?"

I didn't believe for a moment that he meant it. Or, as Holly put it himself, "That'll Be the Day."

Originally appeared in the Duluth News-Tribune & Herald *on Wednesday, August 5, 1987.*

JESSICA LANGE:
LANGE HAS COME A LONG WAY FROM KING KONG

*T*oday a small memoir…

I'm sure actress Jessica Lange would just as soon forget *King Kong*, but I won't. The remake a decade ago of the 1933 horror classic was Lange's first starring role.

As long as the actress is in town this fall making a movie here, I thought I'd recount the night the latest *King Kong* opened in the Twin Ports because I was there and her parents were there and it was the first time her parents ever saw their daughter on the screen.

Word had filtered into this area that a Cloquet "girl" was going to star in the remake of *King Kong*. I was on the arts and entertainment beat at the paper then, and I tried in vain to get information on this Jessica Lange who was going to be in a major movie. We could turn up little more than a photo in the Cloquet High School annual.

At some point before the movie was released, *Time* magazine devoted a cover to *King Kong* and the cover photo showed Lange struggling in the fist of the giant ape. It was the first good look we'd had of the actress who had grown up here. Small biographical bits were pieced together from the *Time* article and other sources, such as people who almost remembered her from high school, but we didn't have much.

When the movie was booked into the Palace Theater in Superior (why it didn't open in Duluth is a mystery), I went to cover the event because there was local interest. Despite that, though, there was no ballyhoo on the opening night. It was just another opening of a movie that had been ballyhooed to death by its producers.

When I arrived, two couples were standing outside the theater and I recognized one of the men as a long-time acquaintance from Moose Lake—Vern Redenbaugh. He introduced me to his wife and their friends, the parents of Jessica Lange.

The Langes were naturally very excited at the prospect of seeing Jessica in a movie. Friendly people, they seemed a little nervous. I tried to interview them before going in, and when we were seated I sat a row behind the star's parents in order to gauge their reaction.

The 1976 *King Kong* became less-than distinguished in an artistic sense, but it was nevertheless a spectacular piece of moviemaking. The big screen, Technicolor and full score make the original version, produced within five years of the advent of sound movies, seem primitive by comparison, although just about everyone agrees the original is better artistically.

But the technological superiority of the modern version made it seem almost overwhelming to her parents when Jessica first appeared on the screen. Here was the girl they had raised suddenly projected larger than life. I took care to watch Mrs. Lange's reaction when Jessica first appeared, and the only word to describe it is flabbergasted.

As I recall it, we all enjoyed the movie as well. It was before the critics got hold of it and told everyone it was trash. In reality, it was an OK adventure film that kept you entertained. Jessica was quite good in it it

seemed to me. She was convincing as anyone could be portraying someone captured by an oversized ape and taken to the top of the World Trade
Center in New York. In the original, the ape and distressed damsel climb
to the top of the Empire State Building.

After it was over, I tried again to interview the Langes, but they were
too dazed to say much. The intervening decade has changed their lives
considerably. That girl in the ape's fist has an Oscar on her mantle now,
and is considered one of the nation's top half-dozen or so film actresses.

But I suspect the Langes will never forget the chilly December night
in Superior when they saw their daughter on film for the very first time.
Thanks to them, I know I won't.

Originally appeared in the Duluth News-Tribune & Herald *on Wednesday, September 30, 1987.*

JFK:

Four Presidential Assassinations in Three Generations

*M*y paternal grandfather, whose life overlapped mine by just two years, was 10 years old when Lincoln was assassinated. In my grandfather's lifetime, two other presidents also were murdered—James Garfield in 1881 and William McKinley in 1901. My father was born 29 years after the Lincoln assassination—a year short of the time that has now elapsed since President John F. Kennedy was shot and killed 30 years ago tomorrow.

In my father's lifetime, two presidents were assassinated: McKinley near the beginning of his life, and Kennedy near the end. He was too young to remember much about McKinley, and I broke the news to him about Kennedy.

Why all this ancient history now? Aside from this being the anniversary of the JFK assassination, it shows that such acts are not quite as rare as we tend to think. Four murdered American presidents in three generations of one family is taking them out at quite a rate.

The day Kennedy was shot, I had been a working journalist for 35 days, counting weekends. Call it a month's experience. Labeling me a journalist at that stage of my career is extravagant. But my title was reporter, and proud of it.

Everyone over five or six years of age on November 22, 1963, remembers what they were doing when they heard Kennedy had been shot in Dallas. A few of us get to share those memories publicly. I share mine to recall my failure to do what I should have done as a newspaper reporter on what was arguably the biggest breaking news story of the century.

I was asleep when the assassination occurred. Working nights on the morning *Duluth News Tribune*, I had already slipped into the out late, sleep late lifestyle of my fellow nightside journalists. So I was still in bed, sound asleep, about 35 minutes past noon that Friday when the ringing of the telephone jolted me awake. It was my aunt, Elsa, who had been watching "As the World Turns" when the soap opera was interrupted with a bulletin that shots had been fired at the president. I clicked on our TV, and CBS had returned to "As the World Turns," but not for long. Within a moment of my tuning in, Walker Cronkite was there in his shirtsleeves confirming that shots had been fired from a grassy knoll and the president's limousine had sped away.

Here are some of my thoughts: *Wow! Big story. Wonder if they know about it down at the paper. You're a reporter, check and see. Don't be silly—of course the newspaper knows. They'd think I was stupid to call and be mad I interrupted them.*

My father was at work as a photo engraver at the newspaper, so I decided to call him. By then it must have been about 12:50 P.M. When my father answered, I said something like, "Boy, big story about Kennedy getting shot, huh?" I phrased it so that, if he already knew, it wouldn't seem like I thought I was breaking the news. But I *was* breaking the news. Busy working on the evening *Duluth Herald*, he said he'd heard nothing about it in the third-floor engraving department.

That made me wonder if I really should call the second-floor newsroom. If they didn't know about it in other parts of the building, maybe the news editors didn't know either. But I didn't call.

I should have called the first time. The *Herald* used to go to press about noon. A normal Friday edition was humming off the press when the assassination occurred. The Associated Press was on top of the story, but they couldn't get printed information out on the wire as quickly as TV networks could interrupt with bulletins.

By the time the *Herald* editors finally received a written bulletin on the wire and literally stopped the presses (the only time in 30 years I've seen that happen), it was about 1 P.M. or shortly after. An hour later, when I arrived for my work shift, I was told that if I had called at, say, 12:40, it would have saved thousands of papers and precious minutes preparing a new *Herald* for that day. "I wish you had called," lamented the news editor. The papers already run off were scrapped and the edition started over with the assassination dominating the front page.

That's my story of the day Kennedy was shot. I'd been in the newspaper business a month and in my own way I had already blown the assassination of a president. Some reporter. Some future.

Originally appeared in the Duluth News-Tribune *on Sunday, November 21, 1993.*

ELVIS PRESLEY:

ELVIS DIDN'T LOOK LIKE A GOD DURING DULUTH VISIT

I am not surprised that many people are turning Elvis worship into an actual religion, as reported recently in this newspaper. It was only a matter of time before the King of Rock 'n' Roll became deified in the minds of many followers. I know a couple of Elvis nuns personally, one a competent bartender.

It could be that in another 50 years, when most of the people on Earth who were occupying the planet when he was alive have gone to be with Elvis, the fervor for an Elvis religion will increase. It is almost impossible to become a god while you are still alive (in anybody's mind but your own and your dog's), or, if you are dead, while people who knew you, or even saw you, are still around.

I could never turn to Elvis as my savior because I saw him in the flesh—not only in performance but up close at the Radisson Hotel, where he stayed when he came to Duluth. At the time I was covering the arts beat for the newspaper and went to cover the first coming of Elvis when he arrived the night before his concert.

In spite of D-Day-like logistical efforts on the part of the Elvis advance party (no one in the group named John the Baptist, though) to keep mortals from seeing the king as he arrived, I was tipped off that he would enter a service door in the hotel, and was waiting by the dumpster when his chauffeured Cadillac pulled in.

Elvis, wearing a knee-length topcoat and racy-looking metal-rimmed glasses, jumped out of the car, halted briefly, gave a beatific smile and disappeared into the hotel with a host of disciples in his entourage. At that late stage of his career, Elvis didn't look like a god, he looked like…oh, never mind. I don't recall seeing any halo, but then I've never been quick to spot halos.

So, having been in his presence, I probably will never be a convert to the Elvis religion, although if they're going to organize one they'll have to come up with more than just Elvis. He should be the center of it, of course, but you've got to have more than the deity. For one thing, you need collection plates.

In order to qualify for official religion, you've got to have an entire hierarchy built up, with the divine one at the top, but lesser personages just below him or her. If this Elvis religion is going to go anywhere, they're simply going to have to make Gladys a saint. Gladys was Elvis' loving mother. She could be depicted holding the baby Elvis in yard displays each Elvismas.

Vernon, Elvis' Earthly father, could be an archangel—the keeper of the gate in the beyond (some religions refer to it as heaven), which they might as well go ahead and call Graceland. That's a natural. Make Col. Tom Parker, Elvis' manager, the other archangel—the Gabriel and Michael of the Elvis religion.

But there's a Priscilla problem. Priscilla is Elvis' ex-wife. It's not good for gods to have ex-wives, but she must be dealt with. Maybe Priscilla could occupy a role similar to Mary Magdelene in Christianity—former bad woman turned good. Not a full saint, though.

By the time Elvisism—let's call it that instead of Elvisianity—gets cranked up at mid-21st Century, Lisa Marie, Elvis' daughter, likely will have gone on to Graceland, too. She should occupy a prominent place in the hierarchy, being the daughter of the deity. But she'd better start behaving, if you can believe the *National Enquirer*.

To round out the religion, I think other prominent rock 'n' rollers should be given high places, even saintships. Certainly Roy Orbison and John Lennon already qualify as saints. Even Conway Twitty, who drifted to country-western after a promising rock 'n' roll start, deserves some standing. Ricky Nelson?

Finally, it's important to remember any successful religion must be dynamic—change with the times. Who knows, Chuck Berry might make a good pope someday. Jerry Lee Lewis? Every religion needs an anti-deity, or devil. Jerry Lee is perfect.

I've got to stop here for space (not outer space) reasons. You can consider what you have read a kind of an Old Testament, Isaiah-style prophecy.

Number the sentences and you've got holy writ.

Originally appeared in the Duluth News-Tribune *on Sunday, January 30, 1994.*

GREGORY PECK:
60 MINUTES WITH ACTOR GREGORY PECK

I have an eight-by-ten glossy photograph showing me standing chatting with Gregory Peck—Duluth's Aerial Lift Bridge in the background.

It was taken by now-retired *News Tribune* staff photographer Karl Jaros in the presidential suite of the Radisson Duluth Hotel. Karl positioned us so the bridge could be seen out the window to give the photo a sense of place.

It was hard to imagine Gregory Peck anywhere outside of Hollywood—except on the movie screen in dozens of memorable roles. My encounter with him was in the mid-1970s, when Peck was in Duluth briefly with his wife on a national tour to promote a movie he'd produced—not starred in—called *The Dove*.

The stately actor, then in his late 50s, said he was phasing out his acting career and thought he'd try producing.

When news of his death last week broke, I found myself thinking back to my 60 minutes with him. I regard it as the most nervous I've ever been as a reporter. Gregory Peck was one of the biggest stars of the sound era—right up there with the older Clark Gable and Gary Cooper. As a lifelong movie fan, it was daunting—almost surreal—to meet this man I'd seen so many times on the screen.

It was arranged that the two of us would have lunch in his hotel suite, during which I could interview him about the movie he had produced. I was a nervous wreck by the time I knocked on his door. He was traveling with his wife, Veronique, and their maid. Peck introduced the two women to me before they stepped into an adjoining room so he and I could have our visit.

I don't remember much about the interview. He ordered roast beef sandwiches from room service. I was so on edge my mouth was dry and I had trouble swallowing. It was like interviewing a monument—his face as familiar as the faces on Mount Rushmore or a portrait on paper currency.

Peck couldn't have been nicer—truly a gentleman. He asked me about my life and wondered if I was related to an old Hollywood reporter by the name of Harold Heffernan. I wasn't. Peck said he'd always liked Harold.

I do remember telling him—and regretting it later—about how as a child my mother took me to *Duel in the Sun* starring Peck, she thinking it was just another western. The following Sunday in church our minister condemned it from the pulpit. The movie featured him in some racy-for-the-day (1946) scenes with Jennifer Jones.

Peck seemed uncomfortable with the idea that one of his movies had been condemned from the pulpit. I can't think of any others that would be. Every pulpit in America should recommend *To Kill a Mockingbird* to anyone who hasn't seen it. And anybody with a romantic bone in their body should see *Roman Holiday*, Audrey Hepburn's first movie and one of Peck's best.

After the interview, I just wanted to get out of there and relax, but Peck insisted we ride down the elevator together (he was heading to

Channel 3 for another interview). Others who got on the elevator as we descended were astonished to encounter Gregory Peck in Duluth. In the lobby, as we shook hands in parting, Peck said, "When you're in Southern California, look us up."

I said something like: "Absolutely, love to, look forward to it, thanks," and high-tailed it out of there.

I never did visit the Pecks in Los Angeles. I'm sure they've wondered why not, all these years.

Originally appeared in the Duluth News Tribune *on Sunday, June 15, 2003.*

JOHNNY CASH:
JOHNNY CASH ON THE BARRELHEAD

I am not a big fan of "country" music in general, although Johnny Cash, who died September 12 at age 71, seemed to be broader than just country or country-rock. Really, he was mostly Johnny Cash, and nobody else was like him.

Fairly early in adult life, I became a classical music snob. After detours into Elvis (he arrived on the scene when I was in high school) and a brief fondness for folk music during college years, I settled into insufferable musical snobbery with almost exclusive interest in classical music.

So while many of my peers were buying records featuring the popular performers of the day, I collected Beethoven symphonies and the works of other classical composers. Couldn't help it; I loved their sound. Still do.

I totally misjudged the Beatles—they're way better than I thought they were when I first ignored them. Bob Dylan? With that voice? I don't think so. Luciano Pavarotti—now that was a voice.

My musical tastes were—and generally are—what most people regard as stuffy. But there's a saying—attributed to several people—that goes, "There are just two kinds of music: good music and bad music." It took me a long time to realize that, and Johnny Cash helped.

Circa 1970 I was city editor of the *News Tribune*, and Cash's show was booked into the Duluth Arena (it wasn't called the DECC in those days) on a Sunday night. My boss, Managing Editor Jack Fein, approached me a few days before the concert and begged me to review it.

I told Fein I was strictly classical, but he pleaded. He had nobody else (who wouldn't demand overtime pay). So I took the two reviewer ducats and that Sunday night my wife and I went to the Johnny Cash show, somewhat reluctantly.

It was a revelation. Of course I'd heard Cash's big hits over the years on TV or radio. You couldn't be alive in America without being aware of gravelly voiced Cash and his music.

On stage with him were his wife, June Carter, her sisters and their mother, Maybelle, legends themselves as The Carter Family, together with a host of backup musicians, including Carl Perkins—a legendary performer in his own right. And topping off the bill was the Statler Brothers quartet ("Flowers on the Wall," "Class of '57," "Whatever Happened to Randolph Scott?").

It was all wonderful, captivating, at times moving. You couldn't help but get caught up in it. The genial Cash, clad in his trademark black outfit (which the New York Times described as "cowboy undertaker") was generous with himself and the other performers.

Cash had appeared in Duluth many times before, including at the Duluth armory in his early days. Maybe he's been back since—I don't know. But that night 30-some years ago, when he was in his prime and he had what seemed like the whole pantheon of country music royalty with him, was pure magic.

It helped to alter my attitudes toward music—broaden them. Surely this man, who reached so many people, was as much an artist as the composers and performers I had embraced.

There are only two kinds of music. Johnny Cash, who couldn't read notes, made good music. So did Luciano Pavarotti, who also is reputed to be fuzzy about note reading.

Originally appeared in the Duluth News Tribune *on Sunday, September 21, 2003.*

Paul Wellstone:
Wellstone Leaves Big Shoes to Fill

*P*aul Wellstone gone? Someone so full of life, of exuberance, of zest, of desire to do good by his fellow man—gone in an instant on a drizzly day right here in the Northland? Can't be, you think. But it's all too true.

I knew Wellstone the way a home-state journalist is likely to know a U.S. Senator. Since he was elected to the Senate, we saw him a couple of times a year. He'd come through for a visit with the editorial board, updating us on what was going on in Washington.

Always upbeat, often passionate about what he believed in, the interviews—chats, really—with Wellstone were something we looked forward to. Politics aside, I liked him personally. I admired his resolve to stand up for what he believed in.

I first met Wellstone in 1982 when he ran for Minnesota state auditor—and lost. Aching to be a major player in the liberal political traditions of his adopted state, the then political science professor at Carleton College in Northfield ran for a state constitutional office, probably seeing it as a stepping stone for bigger and better things to come.

I don't think he'd have made much of a state auditor, although he'd have worked at it. The job would have bored him. Wellstone had bigger things churning in that brain—a passion for helping people who need help and a conviction that government should do what it can to make people's lives better. In short, he was a liberal.

The word liberal has become a pejorative in some (conservative) circles. Those who disliked what Wellstone stood for know he was, perhaps, the most liberal member of the Senate. Wellstone wore that label proudly, unashamedly.

On the occasion of another of our editorial board meetings, after he'd been elected to the Senate, the subject of health care came up. Wellstone felt strongly that America's health care system was broken, and of course he was right. It still isn't fixed. In our conversation—four of us around a table—he became so impassioned about the subject that he began to tear up.

The rest of us, all male, became uncomfortable at his emotional display, but I never forgot it. And, reflecting on it, I could see that was what was best about Wellstone. He really felt what he believed in. He truly was a "bleeding-heart liberal" in the finest sense of that often cynical description. The world needs bleeding-heart liberals, and Wellstone filled that bill almost better than anyone else in a position to help shape American policy.

Finally, on another visit with us, I went to the newspaper's lobby to greet him and guide him to our meeting room, and as we walked up the stairs I noticed that his shoes—loafers—were shot. I mean shot. Hobos heating bean cans over fires in railroad yards had better shoes. Long cracks across the top, exposing his socks beneath, shabby soles.

I kidded him about it, saying something like, "A United States senator can't afford decent shoes?"

Wellstone wasn't a bit abashed. He muttered something about not having time to worry about shoes—too much to do and too little time to do it in. I later wrote a column about the senator's shabby shoes, but I never heard from him about it. Still too busy.

We had another editorial board meeting scheduled with Wellstone, this one Friday afternoon, to talk about the newspaper's endorsement in the Senate race this year. An airplane crash intervened. He was dead, along with his wife and daughter and others on the plane.

As the gray day wore on Friday, and details kept pouring in, for some reason my mind kept going back to those tattered shoes. Who will fill them?

No one quite like Paul Wellstone, whose unlikely life journey took him to the place where his death could affect the balance of the U.S. Senate at a time when the nation appears to be poised for a war he opposed, and when so many other issues remain unresolved that need a committed liberal voice.

Life goes on, but for the time being we'd better put it on hold for a truly good man who was more concerned about providing shoes for those who couldn't afford them than what he wore himself.

Originally appeared in the Duluth News Tribune *on Saturday, October 26, 2002.*

PART VI:

THROUGH THE
REARVIEW MIRROR

THROUGH THE REARVIEW MIRROR

Return with me now to those thrilling—and sometimes not so thrilling—days of yesteryear, when from out of the past come a few first-hand stories, and some passed on by others, that found their way into my columns.

For sheer thrills, try "It Was a Day to Remember," a transcription of my mother's experience in the great 1918 Cloquet fire that blackened much of this region killing hundreds while World War I raged on and the Spanish flu epidemic was taking its toll. And we think times are tough today.

The remainder of the columns in this chapter offer a glimpse of my life that I hope reflect experiences and thoughts many of us share: Christmases past; graduation from high school; cars we have known and loved; even a shake, a rattle and a roll (to save your soul). Cars we have loved? When GM killed off the Oldsmobile, they called it a "grandpa car." Well, find out what the Oldsmobile was before it was a grandpa car in "'Grandpa' Car Had Its Day." Boy, did it ever.

I have included in this chapter a recent Father's Day column that finally, after 75 years, got into print a poem written by my father— "Memories of a Shack at Fond du Lac"—that I always felt deserved broader circulation than framed and on the wall of our home. Reader reaction proved me right—the sentiments expressed and the vernacular of the French voyageur are captivating.

A couple of my own life experiences—shameful behavior on the day I graduated from high school and a tour of my alma mater, UMD, after 45 years—round out this chapter together with my last column for the *Duluth News Tribune*—a sort of summing up of 34 years of column writing for the paper. Happily, the journey continues in *Duluth-Superior Magazine* and my online blog, www.jimheffernan.org, where I continue to write.

NorShor Experience Was Like No Other

*T*he folks hoping to save Duluth's NorShor Theater from eventually suffering the fate of the Palace in Superior (turned to rubble last week) asked me to write something about what it was like to attend a movie at the NorShor in its heyday.

I was born just two years before the building that housed the old Orpheum Theater was gutted and turned into what became the NorShor as we know it. It opened in 1941, and its unique art deco design has been hailed as one of the finest examples of that style. Vestiges of it can still be seen today in the NorShor's present—lamentable—condition almost 25 years after it ceased to exist as a regular theater.

But what was it like to go to a movie there in the days before television, when movies were the principal form of entertainment for most folks? It's been said that 1946 was the peak box-office year for movies in

America. That's about when I started going to movies at the NorShor, accompanied by parents in the early years.

Even to a child, the NorShor was a magical place—at least it was to this child who would rather go to a movie than a ball game any day of the week and twice on Sundays. Duluth had a lot of movie theaters scattered across the downtown and in some outlying neighborhoods, but nothing compared to the NorShor.

Its main entrance was eye-popping, with a hall of mirrors leading from the box office to the auditorium lobby area, which was dominated by a pair of curving staircases leading to the mezzanine and balcony.

Back on the main floor, the auditorium walls featured huge dimly lighted murals—female nudes pausing in a forest glade. Art. Well, art deco.

Before each movie began the screen was shielded by a huge curtain inside the imposing proscenium arch. When the feature was ready to begin, and soundtrack music rose, the movie's image would be projected at first on the curtain, which, in a few seconds, would be drawn back revealing the screen. When the movie was over, as "The End" flashed on the screen, the curtain would glide shut.

I've heard that the owners had to keep a member of the union representing stagehands employed at the theater just to open and close the curtain.

No other theater in Duluth even attempted such pageantry or had such class. It made going to movies at the NorShor really special, like dining in a fine restaurant versus stopping by a café for a blue-plate special.

In my experience, after the movie, we'd often peruse the paintings in the narrow but sizable art gallery off the main downstairs lobby where local artists and photographers would display their works.

Still, you were there just to see a movie, even if it was in a unique setting. Once the lights went down and the curtain opened, the NorShor was just like any other movie house, but somehow the lavish surroundings enhanced your enjoyment.

All of this cost the theater's operators money, of course, which was probably why the NorShor charged more than some others movie houses for kids—12 cents. A child could get into the Lyceum for 9 cents.

Originally appeared in the Duluth News Tribune *on Sunday, November 19, 2006.*

IT TAKES A PILLAGE TO SAVE A SOUL

Get out in the kitchen and rattle them pots and pans.

Get out in the kitchen and rattle them pots and pans...

Gotta shake, rattle and roll, gotta shake, rattle and roll, gotta shake, rattle and roll, gotta shake, rattle and roll;

You never do nuthin' to save your doggone soul.

Well, you could go to church on Easter Sunday to save your doggone soul. Not that there are any assurances.

I heard the '50s anthem "Shake, Rattle and Roll" on an oldies radio station last week. I came of age in the '50s, just when such music started shaking and rattling the foundations of "traditional" America, whatever that was. Elvis hit then, too, and somehow, in so many ways, this country has never been the same.

My upbringing was deeply rooted in the Scandinavian Lutheran tradition flowing out of the 19th century. Very conservative lifestyles. Just about everything was a sin, it seemed to me. You want to sin? Join some other religion. You want eternal salvation? Be a Lutheran, especially a Swedish Lutheran. Don't smoke, drink, dance, play cards, go to movies on Sunday, wear much makeup, dress too fancy, or embrace pop culture— especially pop music. And keep your nose clean. Cuss? How'd you like a large order of soap for lunch?

Shake, rattle and roll, indeed.

It was confusing, let me tell you. On the one hand, you wanted to be a good Lutheran boy; on the other, you wanted to fit in with your generation.

It led to a sort of informal separation of church and state of being. Pious behavior around your parents and church people, acting out in other ways among your friends. What other ways? Oh, the usual kid stuff: pillage, burglary, robbery, debauchery, breaking of the speed limit, parking in bus stops, spitting on the sidewalk, leaving spearmint gum on the bedpost overnight. Well, maybe not burglary and robbery.

If you were going to rock around the clock you better hope that nobody from church would see you. Of course the almighty was watching, no matter what. Keep *that* in mind, junior.

So now, 50 years later, I look back on this dichotomy with a good deal of fondness, amusement and nostalgia.

Thanks to the church, at the time I thought I was a wild kid, skulking around in a leather jacket, sneaking a smoke when nobody was looking, driving up and down the streets in hot rods with rumbling exhaust systems, drag racing with whoever's next to you at traffic signals, hanging around pool halls. (Surely billiards was a sin.)

Not exactly the 19th century Scandinavian Lutheran tradition.

But it remained, though, on Sunday mornings, especially Easter Sunday mornings. The dressing up in new clothes for Easter service, the communion rail lined with white lilies, the pipe organ blasting joyous anthems of the resurrection, the choirs, the hymns, the hopeful message, the benediction. You better believe the Lord was in his holy temple.

Once years ago when I was a news reporter covering police, just for the heck of it I asked the officer in charge of the records bureau to check out my police file. There was no file. They never heard of me. Some wild kid.

Now I'm at the stage of life where you wonder about where you stand in the big file upstairs. Jeepers. What if they have no file?

I'd better go to church today. Gotta do sumpin' to save my dog-gone soul.

Originally appeared in the Duluth News Tribune *on Sunday, March 27, 2005.*

SOMETIMES LIFE'S A RAT SHOOT

When I walked out the door of Duluth Denfeld High School on the night I graduated, I knew life had many options. To start with, my parents were hosting a small party of relatives in honor of me in our home, so naturally I didn't want to go to that.

My immediate friends faced a similar problem. Now that we were out of high school and grown up, we had to get on with our lives and had no time for small gatherings of relatives in the home. We had other things to do.

What we did that night was go to a garbage dump in Gary-New Duluth. Oh, I swung by the house for a few minutes, said "Hi" to the guests, collected the cards containing money they gave me and ducked back out. I had better things to do. That would include the Gary dump.

Why we picked the Gary dump, I'm not sure today, as I reminisce about these matters. Somebody said they'd be shooting rats there. That certainly sounded a lot better than sitting around the living room of your house with proud loved ones and other relatives there to honor you and give you money.

Besides, we were high school graduates. We were liberated from the mundane family kinds of things and it was our turn to make our marks on the world. So on that night we—that's me and my immediate friends—graduated, we went to the Gary dump to watch the ritual killing of rats.

Is shining headlights on garbage piles and shooting rats with .22s ritual killing? It might be if you go to a ceremony wearing a robe and march in step to rhythmical music with a bunch of other people before you do it.

I didn't shoot rats myself that night almost 30 Junes ago. I don't think anyone in our car even had a gun. We were just there to *watch* rat killing on this night when we had graduated from high school. The procession was over, the music had ended, the speeches had been made (*And now as you go forth into the world to watch rats get shot...*), the diplomas handed out, the handshakes shaken, and we were in the Gary dump watching rats die. My folks, aunts, uncles, cousins and other people who cared about me were at my house honoring me and I was at a rat shoot.

I sometimes wonder what it meant that I went to a rat kill at a garbage dump on the night I was graduated. I was still in my blue graduation suit there at the dump. I was now a high school grad, after all.

Now all these years later, in pondering what it meant, I have decided that my going to a garbage dump to watch rat shooting that night meant nothing. I've decided that it was merely stupid, which is the prerogative of a fresh high school graduate of 17.

It is with people who shared some of these truly stupid experiences that many of us gather this summer for a class reunion, and I sometimes wonder why.

But if they ever have a reunion of the gang that used to shoot rats, or watch rats get shot, at the Gary dump, I won't be there.

I'd rather be home with relatives, so I guess I've finally grown up.

Originally appeared in the Duluth News-Tribune & Herald *circa July, 1986.*

UMD REVISITED

I went back to college last week and felt a little like Rodney Dangerfield in *Back to School,* one of my favorite campus movies after *Animal House.*

Actually, I only visited UMD, where I was a student during the Eisenhower/Kennedy administrations when men were men and boys were boys and girls were—well, I don't know. I never understood them very well. They were quite chaste but not quite as chaste as I thought they were at the time.

Talk about back to the future, though. Living here all these years, I have returned to the University of Minnesota Duluth campus many times to attend plays or even talk to classes. But last week I was there to visit out-of-town friends staying at a UMD residence hall for the summer, and got a chance to wander around a bit. A lot of folks who remember the Eisenhower administration stay at UMD in the summer, and maybe a few Truman and Roosevelts as well.

It's a stark contrast with new students who were arriving for freshmen orientation as we wandered around the campus, sticking our noses into rooms that were actually there when we were students. This year's freshman class has memories going all the way back to the Clinton administration when boys were boys and girls—well, never mind.

One of the friends I was visiting attended UMD when I did. We did a lot of reminiscing about our college years which, we now agree, we didn't take seriously enough in an academic sense. We recalled our bad-old tendency to pay almost no attention to classroom instruction, and depend on our innate, vast knowledge of the world and everything in it to get through exams. One time I got a D in a natural science course and was advised by a family member to complain to the professor. I registered my complaint and the professor said, "Mr. Heffernan, you have no idea how lucky you are that you got a D."

Well, there went medical school.

Actually, I wasn't aiming at medical school anyway. I wanted to be in the theater, which is why I never tried out for any plays. But that was due to the advice of my freshman adviser, a professor of theater. When he asked what I was interested in, I openly confessed that I'd always loved the theater, thinking he'd invite me to join the college acting troupe, and Broadway or Hollywood could not be far behind. Instead, the professor frowned dramatically and told me to take geography.

So there went Broadway and Hollywood.

I did take geography, but didn't do that well there, either. My lifelong confusion over which is latitude and which is longitude counted me out as an up-and-coming geographer, both the professor and I learned very quickly.

I finally found refuge in the English department where the classes were more to my liking and the professors wore better tweed. You got to read a whole bunch of books by famous authors, which sure beat poring over geography texts or dissecting unfortunate stray cats and spotted frogs.

Still, my visiting friend and I agreed last week that it would be fun to be 18 again and start college all over. We'd do things differently, that's for sure—buckle down and really hit the books and maybe, just maybe, if we were lucky, some day retire and come back and stay in a UMD dorm in the summer.

There went a lifetime.

Originally appeared in the Duluth News Tribune *on Sunday, August 20, 2006.*

"Grandpa" Car Had Its Day

*S*o now there will be no Oldsmobile. I could take the end of Plymouth, but Oldsmobile?

When GM announced the demise of the Oldsmobile last week it was like somebody drove a stake of holly through my heart.

Oldsmobile, the dream car of my youth, the object of my teenage reveries. Pay no attention to the news stories saying Oldsmobile had such a stodgy image that "no one 45 and younger wants to be seen driving an Oldsmobile." That might be true of today's Oldsmobiles.

But the stories fail to mention the halcyon days of Oldsmobile when it was *the* car of youth, probably the most exciting car of the '50s until Chevy got a V-8 in '55 and left everything else in its dust.

Nothing compared to the Oldsmobiles of the first half of the 1950s. They were fast and they were gorgeous. The 1954 Oldsmobile Holiday with its lightning-like side chrome was a car to quit school for. I knew people who did: They went to work on the dusty mason gang at the steel plant to make payments on a '54 or '55 Olds.

I never had one of those cars. Too poor, or too lazy to go out and work for one or too stupid to quit school.

Oldsmobiles pulled ahead of the pack after the war, about '48 or '49, when they equipped them with a V-8 engine and hydromatic transmission. That was the only automatic transmission of the day that could compare with a stick. The rest were slushy—Buick's Dynaflow, Chevrolet's Power Glide, Ford's Ford-O-Matic, Mercury's Merc-O-Matic.

Oh, wow. I just read what I've written so far and I'm afraid I've lost most of the women, all of the men under 50, and every dog, cat or mule that reads the *News Tribune*. What do they care about Oldsmobile? I care.

If you live long enough you see a lot of things change that you thought would be around forever. I'm of a generation that thought Studebaker, Hudson, DeSoto and Packard would be around forever.

So now Oldsmobile is on its way to joining the ranks of those forgotten nameplates in extinction, except for a few collectors' cars taken out for summer parades.

But before it goes, let the record show that Oldsmobile was not always a "grandpa" car at all. In an era when a drag race could occur at any stoplight, and often did, almost nothing was faster off the line than an Olds Super 88 in '52, '53, '54 and '55. And if you wanted to go up to the Miller Trunk and cruise at 110-plus or race almost anybody else to see whose top end was fastest, you took one of those Oldsmobiles.

Or if you wanted to cruise down to the roller rink on a hot summer night to offer your services to girls without a ride home, nothing got them into the car like an Oldsmobile. Grandpa car, indeed. There are plenty of grandpas around today *because* of those Oldsmobiles.

Originally appeared in the Duluth News Tribune *on Sunday, December 17, 2000.*

MEMORIES OF A SHACK AT FOND DU LAC

*O*ver the years I've generally avoided writing about anything personal, seldom mentioning family members' real names or recounting actual events, but this Father's Day I'm making an exception because—who knows?—it could be my last chance to share a deeply personal family anecdote involving my own father.

My late parents, George and Ruth, were married 74 years ago last month in Duluth. For the first few months of their life together they settled in a cabin on the hillside overlooking the western Duluth neighborhood of Fond du Lac, the tiny picturesque hamlet on the bend in the St. Louis River where it begins to separate Minnesota and Wisconsin.

I don't know much about the history of Fond du Lac, other than it is said it was the site of a 17th century fur-trading post when this part of the world was the territory of France.

Many older Duluthians recall a replica of that fur trading post and small fort that stood for many years in Chambers Grove Park, at the western end of Fond du Lac. Our church used to have its annual Sunday school picnic there, complete with a makeshift pulpit and portable pump organ, which my mother played for the hymn singing.

When I was a child, each June, as we passed through Fond du Lac on the drive to the picnic, my parents would look up on the hillside and point to the little cabin where they had spent the first few months of their married life in 1932. Such things are of little interest to a child, looking forward to the picnic. But you pick up on things your parents say and do nevertheless, and, as you grow into adulthood yourself, these snippets of family history stick with you.

So it's not surprising that these many years later I think of that honeymoon cabin when I drive through Fond du Lac, and I ruminate about how my father must have been taken with the village's long history as he and my mother enjoyed the first few months of their life together. It inspired him to write a poem that survives in the family archives that I share with you on this Father's Day because I hope it has merit beyond just the family and can be appreciated by anyone.

Because of Fond du Lac's storied association with the French voyageurs, he wrote it in what he hoped sounded like a Frenchman expressing himself in English. So the misspellings are intended to reflect what he thought of as a French/English dialect. The poem has no title; it just starts with these words:

> Up in the shack at Fond du Lac
> I took my bran new wife.
> We sing a song as we go along,
> An tink of a happy life.
>
> I swear by de honor of Jean du Lhut
> An my mother who swore by me,
> I follow de trail good men take
> Thru dis world of mystery.

So long I live, jus so long I give,
To they who most need me,
And play de game, to all de same,
Dat make good historee.

When I am old, trail's end is near,
Tho wit weary bones I track,
An the setting sun seems close to me,
Cause life is in de back.

Yet wit happiness I still shall go,
When I tink of my shack…
At Fon du Lac.

The trail ended for George in 1971. Last time I checked, the cabin was still there.

Originally appeared in the Duluth News Tribune *on Sunday, June 18, 2006.*

A Light That Will Never Fail

*I*f you were brought up close to a church, as I was, it will always hold a special place in your heart, especially at Christmas. Even if you've moved on to other churches, or away from religion entirely, that church of your childhood is where many of your Christmas memories still reside.

Even though fully a half century separates me today from those memories of Christmases past, they seem as real as if they occurred just last Christmas.

Christmases in my adulthood seem to run together, making it difficult to distinguish one from another. Not so, the Christmases of my childhood. As with the scenes of his early life shown to Scrooge by the Ghost of Christmas Past, I can picture with great detail my childhood church at Christmas.

First of all, there were the trees at the front of the sanctuary, two of them, one on each side of the altar, rising to somewhere above the rail of the balcony that encircled the sanctuary. The sill of every stained-glass sanctuary window held candles and a spray of pine. Swags of evergreen festooned the balcony rail and a huge wreath encircled the clock. A pair of manger scenes were affixed to the towering organ pipes on either side of the choir loft; still tableaux of Mary and Joseph and the Christ Child.

To the eyes of a child, this was a scene of wonder, of awe. Candles flickered everywhere and the sanctuary shimmered in an amber glow.

The church of my childhood was founded in Duluth's West End in the 1880s by Swedish immigrants meeting first in other buildings before constructing a large brick edifice, with a tall cross-topped steeple, shortly after the turn of the last century.

These people, and their sons and daughters born in the United States, took their Christmases seriously. By the time I came along some 40 years after the church was built, the traditions were well established with elaborate Sunday school Christmas programs, special music services put on by the three choirs and even an early Christmas morning service in the Swedish language for the old guard.

After the Sunday school program (enactment of the classic manger scene included), each child received boxes of Christmas hard candy and other goodies. Adult church societies, women's and men's, held Christmas gatherings in the parlors.

Now all of the old guard, and many of the following generation as well, have gone on to that place they worked so hard to glorify in this small corner of Christendom. Still another generation, the one taking us into these times, has held forth bravely, although the church membership is diminished, even as its neighborhood has changed.

Now I'm told the future of Bethany Lutheran Church is uncertain.

Few things last more than 100 years in the same place. Three of its Roman Catholic neighbors have been consolidated into one new building.

Still, if this church—once so strong, so seemingly indestructible as a bastion against the forces of darkness—must go the way of its founders, let it not be forgotten.

As long as there is breath left in me, it will remain the place where the wonder of this joyous season was first given light; where the glow will remain indistinguishable, if only as a warm memory of a time long past.

Originally appeared in the Duluth News Tribune *on Sunday, December 23, 2001.*

THAT SPECIAL CHRISTMAS PLACE

*I*t happens to everyone sooner or later, and this year it's my turn. I lasted longer than most—not as long as some. This is the first year there will be no Christmas in the home I grew up in.

Many people my age—commonly called "middle"—have only memories of the home where they spent their first Christmas and Christmases thereafter throughout their childhood. Others lived in several places during those years—often in different cities.

But we're a consistent lot, and our family home stayed intact for close to 45 years, in spite of the loss of my father a dozen years ago and the moving away and marrying of the two boys. This fall we lost our mother, and there will be no more Christmases in that home for us.

I have come to believe that part of the warmth of Christmas felt by most of us when we grow up is rooted in memories of childhood Christmases—happy memories made bittersweet by the passage of time and passing of the people who populated them. And I am coming to understand how Dickens chose ghosts in his "Christmas Carol" to represent his three Christmases.

In a stop last week at the old family home, bereft of holiday decorations for the first time, ghosts of Christmases past—dozens of them—shimmered before my eyes...the place in front of the window where we used to place the tree...the big mirror that used to be festooned with garlands...the dining room table that was always decorated with candles.

As I stood in the hall of the now unoccupied house—framed pictures of family members placed here and there in the main rooms—the sights, sounds and smells of Christmases past, even as recently as a year ago, rushed back for a moment. Our balsam, close to nine feet tall, was there in front of the window, its familiar ornaments shimmering in the colored lights. Gifts encircled its foot and were stacked knee high. The aroma of foods only prepared at Christmastime—Scandinavian sylta, potato sausage, fruitcake, special cookies—wafted from the kitchen.

The sounds of laughter, the tearing of wrappings and voices "Hey, just what I wanted!" "Thanks a million!" "I love it!" filled the room. And above the din, the sound of a well-played piano, full bass chords resounding, treble ringing, "O come, all ye faithful..." and later, a hushed "Silent Night." We will never hear that piano played that way again.

This year Christmas is not calling on that home except in the memories of those of us who spent so many there that it will always be *the* Christmas place for us no matter where we live.

In every life where Christmas comes at all, there is that one place from childhood where it will live forever. We were lucky to have such a Christmas place for as long as we did.

Originally appeared in the Duluth News-Tribune & Herald *on Sunday, December 25, 1983.*

IT WAS A DAY TO REMEMBER

*T*oday marks the 70th anniversary of the great Cloquet fire that burned much of Northeastern Minnesota and killed hundreds of people. The ranks of those who remember it first-hand are getting thin, although there are still plenty of people in their late 70s and older around to tell about it.

Mention of the Cloquet fire brings vivid memories to me. While I missed it by more than two decades, my mother, Ruth Carlson, was age 19 and not yet married on that October 12, 1918, and talked of it often when I was growing up.

Everybody who was in this area then had a story to tell about that terrible day. Many have passed the stories down through their families. This is my mother's Cloquet fire, as she told the story often, once, a couple of years before she died in 1983, into a tape recorder.

They say that to a foot soldier huddled in a foxhole in combat the war is only as big as that foxhole. So it is with witnesses of cataclysmic events. We only see a small part and only after they are over do we learn of their scope.

My mother's Cloquet fire story started in downtown Duluth and ended in her home on Piedmont Avenue between Third and Fourth streets in the West End. Here, in her words, is the way it was—for her.

"It was a very lovely sunshiny day. It was a Saturday and I had baked several loaves of bread. My friend and I went downtown in the afternoon to look for a birthday gift for another friend. We left about 2:30 and went to Wahl's store, which was George A. Gray Company then.

"(After shopping) when we came out on Superior Street a terrific wind was blowing and it was very dark. We boarded a streetcar and coming up Piedmont Avenue we met trucks with people on them screaming. Balls of fire were rolling down the avenue, paper and other debris burning. We were frightened and hurried to our homes. (At that point) we hadn't heard what had happened.

"The wind was so strong you could hardly breathe. I got home and my family was very excited. My mother had died in April so it was my father and five (younger) sisters wondering where to go. People were driving down Piedmont Avenue in trucks and cars, screaming. They had been picked up in Hermantown where everything was on fire.

"Soon a friend of ours called and told us to pack clothes and a little food and be ready to flee down to the bay because Duluth was surrounded by fire and (he said) the bridge crossing to Superior was burning. The Woodland area was also burning. A neighbor came over crying and wringing her hands because her three children were visiting in Lakewood with their grandmother. She didn't know if they were alive.

"Then we heard they had ordered the people from Twelfth to Tenth streets and the area all around there to vacate. There was so much smoke we could hardly breathe. The rooms were filled with smoke. They called my dad and asked if he would take the grocery truck from where he worked to Hermantown to pick up people. He couldn't leave us alone.

"(Later in the evening) my younger sisters were sleeping and my dad and I were up watching. About 2 o'clock in the morning the wind died down. We were saved—how thankful we were. My friend and I walked up to Hermantown the next day. What a sight we saw—people weeping standing in front of ash piles that had been their homes…so much sickness, too…the people were dying from the flu. (The fire occurred during the great Spanish flu epidemic.) It was not a pretty sight to see beautiful trees and vegetation all black, but the people were brave and went back to their small farms and started to build again.

"It was a day to remember."

I have one other family account of that fire. My father (who had not yet met my mother) was in the Army (World War I was winding down), stationed in San Francisco. He knew nothing of the fire in his hometown until newspapers reported it with front page headlines proclaiming such things as "Duluth Leveled By Fire."

It was some time before he could determine his own parents and siblings back in Duluth had survived, and most of Duluth itself had not burned.

Originally appeared in the Duluth News-Tribune & Herald *on Wednesday, October 12, 1988.*

To All the Words I've Left Behind

*T*his is my last column for the *Duluth News Tribune*. The newspaper has decided it wants to feature other voices on this page. So be it.

The metrics are interesting—at least to me. I was 34 years old when I started this column. I am now 68. So I have been writing this column for half my lifetime. The columns average some 600 words each, and I averaged about 50 a year. That produces about 30,000 words per year. In 34 years, it amounts to some 1,020,000 words.

The infamously long Russian novel *War and Peace* contains 560,000 words in English translation. So total word count of these columns is a few under *War and Peace* doubled. No wonder they made Tolstoy a count.

Lots of words, lots of fun, sometimes lots of struggle to come up with ideas. Many people have asked where I get my ideas, and I always say the same thing: "In the shower." Some showed it—all wet.

But so many readers over the years have been supportive, writing me, coming up to me on the street, calling, e-mailing. They have no idea how gratifying that has been, and I thank them.

Before I depart these pages, I should sew up a few loose ends, one of them involving mean-old Blanche, always identified as the little big woman at our house who sat around all day in a recliner wearing a muu-muu, smoking cigarettes and munching munchies. I still frequently get asked what became of Blanche.

Blanche drowned several years ago in a sea of political correctness. But she had a great sendoff. She was carried off in a coffin that resembled a package of Virginia Slims and hoisted onto a flatbed truck with a forklift driven by a guy in a tuxedo borrowed from a symphony contrabassoon player. There wasn't a wet eye in the crowd when the crane lowered her into her final resting place, the kids being in the penitentiary.

Then there's the Ethnic Editor—that's me. I have always been proud to be the Dean of Twin Ports ethnic editors; but we are a dying breed. With the newspaper industry in decline, I doubt that an ethnic editor will be appointed to succeed me. It means, of course, that our good Northland Swedes will have to defend themselves against the slings and arrows of those uppity Norwegians without any help from me. Lots of luck.

Finally, I sign off with the last two verses of a poem I wrote years ago that turned out to be the most popular column of all 1,700 of them. It was called "Cooler Near the Lake," which needs no elaboration. Here's how it ended:

> I know the day is coming when
> The real God's country beckons,
> And when St. Peter meets me there,
> He'll ask my home, I reckon.
> And when I tell him it's Duluth,
> He'll say, "For heaven's sake,
> Ain't that the place everyone says
> Is cooler near the lake?"

"That's it," I'll cry, "oh kindly saint,
And in this realm please spare,
From chilly off-lake breezes,
And winter underwear."
"If it's heat you want," he'll reply,
"In the other place you'll bake."
"Fine, send me any place except
Where it's cooler near the lake."

Amen.

Originally appeared in the Duluth News Tribune *on Sunday, June 22, 2008.*

ABOUT THE AUTHOR

Jim Heffernan is a proud native of Duluth, Minnesota. He grew up in Duluth's West End and attended Lincoln Elementary and Junior High School and Denfeld High School before receiving his B.A. in Social Sciences and English from the University of Minnesota Duluth in 1962.

Following active service in the U.S. Army, Jim began his journalism career at the *Duluth News Tribune* and *Duluth Herald* in 1963. He served as a general assignment reporter, education reporter, city government reporter, *News Tribune* city editor, arts and entertainment writer/editor, and associate editor of the editorial pages in a career spanning 42 years.

For 34 years he also wrote a humor and "slice of life" column for the Duluth newspapers, which he continued—after retiring from full-time employment at the newspaper in 2005—until June 2008. He currently writes a monthly column for *Duluth-Superior Magazine* and maintains a blog at www.jimheffernan.org.

As a member of the *Duluth News Tribune's* editorial board and staff, he has contributed to editorials that have received several state awards. He also won a first place Minnesota Society of Professional Journalists award for a column about Hubert Humphrey, and in 1989 was presented a Distinguished Alumni Award by the University of Minnesota Duluth.

Jim lives in Hermantown with his wife, Voula, and together they are the proud parents of of Kate Heffernan Carson and Patrick Heffernan and grandparents of Paige and Jack Carson and twins Ben and Nick Heffernan and their new sibling, Ashton Patrick Heffernan, who was born just in time to get his name in this book.

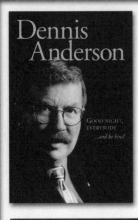